THE

PARENTS'

PLAN FOR

OVERCOMING

CHILDHOOD

OBESITY

D0088566

BST

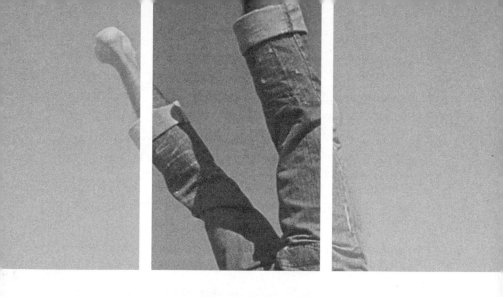

THE NO-GIMMICK GUIDE TO

RAISING FIT KIDS

ROBERT S. ANDERSEN, M.D.

Tyndale House Publishers, Inc.
CAROL STREAM, ILLINOIS

A Focus on the Family book published by Tyndale House Publishers, Carol Stream, Illinois 60188

TYNDALE and Tyndale's quill logo are registered trademarks of Tyndale House Publishers, Inc.

The author is represented by the literary agency of Flair Communications, 1002 Highmoor Road, Lombard, Illinois 60148.

Cover photographs: girl performing a cartwheel © by Zastavkin/istockphoto; cucumbers © by Annette Linnea/istockphoto; kiwi © by Meltonmedia/istockphoto; peas © by istockphoto; man in handstand © by Veer; girl in handstand © by Photis/Jupiter Images. All rights reserved.
Cover design: Ron Kaufmann

Library of Congress Cataloging-in-Publication Data
Andersen, Robert S. (Robert Scott), 1959-
   The no-gimmick guide to raising fit kids : the parents' plan for overcoming childhood obesity / Robert S. Andersen.
      p. cm. — (Focus on the Family)
   Includes bibliographical references and index.
   ISBN-13: 978-1-58997-379-4
   ISBN-10: 1-58997-379-8
   1. Obesity in children—Prevention—Popular works. I. Title. II. Series: Focus on the Family book
   RJ399.C6A53 2006
   618.92'398—dc22

                                           2006017914

Printed in the United States of America
1 2 3 4 5 6 7 8 9 / 11 10 09 08 07 06

This book is dedicated to my loving wife and family,
wonderful patients, and outstanding colleagues and staff.

CONTENTS

PART SIX
CHANGING YOUR CHILD'S LIFESTYLE

PART SEVEN
MAINTAINING MOMENTUM

EPILOGUE

ABOUT THE AUTHOR

Dr. Robert Andersen is a pediatrician in the Chicago area. The Consumers' Research Council of America, based in Washington, D.C., named him one of "America's Top Pediatricians" for 2004-2005 and 2005-2006.

Dr. Andersen graduated from the University of Illinois College of Medicine in 1985. He completed his residency in pediatrics at Phoenix Children's Hospital and Maricopa Medical Center in Phoenix, Arizona. Named the Outstanding Intern of the Year after completing his first year, he was appointed a chief resident for his final year.

After four years in Phoenix, he returned to his native Chicago to practice at the Elmhurst Clinic, a multi-specialty group in Elmhurst, Illinois, where he has practiced ever since. His grandfather, pediatrician Ernest Watson, was a founder of the clinic.

Dr. Andersen has served as chairman of the Department of Pediatrics both at the Elmhurst Clinic and Elmhurst Memorial Hospital. Board-certified by the American Board of Pediatrics, he is a fellow of the American Academy of Pediatrics and the American College of Pediatricians.

A former basketball and baseball player in high school, a walk-on for the University of Illinois varsity basketball team practice squad in 1977, and scratch golfer, Dr. Andersen has long had an interest in sports, the outdoors, and fitness. He also serves as an elder, assistant pastor, and Bible teacher under Pastor Peter Philippi at Grace Bible Church of Rolling Meadows in Rolling Meadows, Illinois.

Dr. Andersen and his wife, Cheryl, reside in a Chicago suburb. They have two daughters, Heather (Carson) and Jamie, and a son-in-law, Tyler.

ACKNOWLEDGMENTS

Special thanks go to the following friends and colleagues for their time and expertise in reviewing the manuscript and making helpful suggestions: Jessica Krauser, B.A., A.C.E., former fitness program manager and current personal trainer at the Wheaton Sport Center, Wheaton, Illinois; and Don Hoffman, M.D., and Julie Lopatka, M.D., of the Elmhurst Clinic Department of Pediatrics, Elmhurst, Illinois.

NOTE

This book is intended as an aid for parents attempting to help a child struggling with obesity, and a preventative guide to help parents avoid the problem of obesity. The facts herein have been carefully researched, drawn from the latest medical and nutritional literature. They are not intended, however, to be a substitute for the care and personal advice of your physician.

Examples cited in the book are based on actual patients. Names and other details have been altered to ensure their privacy.

The author has no financial ties to any product or franchise mentioned in this book, and has not received remuneration from any company or product mentioned.

A CAUTION FOR PARENTS

Excessive weight is jeopardizing the well-being of many of our children. We need to squarely face the problem of obesity and poor nutrition in our society.

But we must never forget—nor allow our children to forget—that what really counts in life is character. What we are on the inside is far more important than our outward appearance.

Character has been defined as what we do when no one is looking. Our actions reflect the thoughts of our minds, what the Bible calls our "heart." God is concerned with our hearts, the seats of our true identities. First Samuel 16:7 says, "For the LORD does not see as man sees; for man looks at the outward appearance, but the LORD looks at the heart." Proverbs 4:23 adds, "Keep your heart with all diligence, for out of it spring the issues of life."

The world glorifies appearances and possessions; God values character. Many people appear fulfilled and beautiful on the outside, but are lonely and unattractive on the inside. The converse can be equally true.

Both adults and children are easily pulled into the deception that outward appearances are all-important. As we discuss the problem of obesity, let's remember that we're concerned with the negative *health* implications of being overweight. God infinitely loves both us and the children we're trying to help; they need to know that fact more than any other.

While we strive to optimize our children's physical health, let's not forget to work toward making certain that their hearts are fit, too. Only then will they truly be ready to serve God optimally in whatever they do—thus living life to the fullest.

INTRODUCTION

When I was growing up, overweight children were a rarity. Like "Fat Albert," the famous Cosby Kids character, they stood out in a crowd.

Not anymore. We're in the midst of a staggering surge of obesity among the most precious of our society. If the trend isn't reversed, the consequences will be dire.

How do we know this? The Centers for Disease Control and Prevention, part of the U.S. government's Department of Health and Human Services, has a research arm called the National Center for Health Statistics. Since 1971 it's tracked obesity rates in the U.S., and is the source of much of our knowledge on the subject.

The most recent survey was taken in 1999-2000. It showed a dramatic increase in the prevalence of childhood obesity during the last 20 years. In 1980, about 5 percent of American children and adolescents were obese. In 2000 the rate was approximately 10 percent for children ages 2-5, and about 15 percent for those ages 6-19. Rates are much higher in certain ethnic populations; African-American, Latino, and Native American children suffer obesity rates as high as 35 percent.

Increases like these in such a short time are unprecedented. Obesity rates in kids have almost tripled in the last 20 years! Adults fare no better—and serve as poor role models for their offspring.

Not only are we seeing more bodily obesity, but in my opinion we're also witnessing a decline in our kids' fitness of mind. Just as video games, computers, and TV have led to less physical exercise, the mass media have lulled some of our kids into an intellectual and spiritual lassitude. Is there a connection?

Despite the strides our society has made toward accepting adults and children as they are, the stigma of obesity continues to carry negative psychosocial consequences. I've seen looks of despair on children's faces, and heard their stories of rejection. Along with sadness, it angers me to see how some of these kids are treated.

The physical ramifications of obesity are no less daunting. Many of these children will face a lifetime of obesity-related problems—and a significantly shortened lifespan. As they grow older, we'll see increased rates of diabetes, heart disease, cancer, and joint disease. Obesity in all age groups, and particularly in children, poses a public health crisis that will seriously affect the well-being of the world. It's possible that this generation of children may be the first to live shorter lives than their parents, due to the complications of obesity.

The financial impact is ominous as well. A 2004 study published in the journal *Obesity Research*[1] estimated that in 2003, obesity-related health care costs in the U.S. reached $75 *billion,* with taxpayers on the hook for about $38 billion of that total (Medicare and Medicaid's share). This annually increasing amount of money will have to come from somewhere, and taxpayers can pony up only so much before significantly slowing the economy. As more and more money goes to rising health costs, less will be available for other worthy causes.

Obesity rates aren't just a problem in the U.S., either. In the U.K., as of 2001, estimates were that about 8.5 percent of 6-year-olds and about 15 percent of 15-year-olds were obese.[2] In 2000, the World Health Organization gave obesity epidemic status.

There's no evidence that this epidemic has slowed in the ensuing years. On the contrary, my eyes tell me it's only picking up speed. If the U.S. can find ways to gain control of its obesity epidemic, this information will be very helpful to the rest of the world.

For a pediatrician, there may be no more frustrating problem than obesity. The issue is so multifaceted—shaped by physical, social, societal, family, psychological, spiritual, nutritional, and other factors—even the most experienced practitioner can be quickly overwhelmed.

Our window of opportunity to render assistance as physicians is narrow. If a child is still overweight in the teen years, the rate of successful long-term weight loss is low. Often we simply lack the time or resources to deal effectively with obesity. And so many others—parents, other relatives, schools, friends—must be involved in the effort that victory over the problem is uncommon.

One mom recently told me that she and her daughter had made substantial changes at home to begin slimming down. But her ex-husband and in-laws were telling the child that there was no problem—she could eat what she wanted as long as she exercised. Needless to say, this seven-year-old was confused. Yet this is not an unusual scenario.

Things must change. That's why, after 18 years of pediatric practice in the trenches, caring for many overweight children, I saw the need for a simple guide for parents who want to help their children conquer obesity and grow up to be fit and healthy. No responsible parent wants less for his or her child, and no physician should settle for any other outcome.

Since the best "cure" is prevention, I've also designed this book to help parents of young children avoid the mistakes leading to obesity. The goal is to keep your children from becoming overweight, and to teach them healthy eating habits and activity levels from a young age.

Though I'll touch briefly on disease conditions that cause obesity, this book deals mainly with "common"—or what we in the medical field call "exogenous"—obesity. A few obese children may suffer from as-yet-undefined genetic mutations of appetite control mechanisms, but most are simply eating too much.

What about hopes for "wonder drugs" that could control appetite or render calories powerless? There are some interesting developments in the study of obesity, ones that may lead to some pharmacologic therapies in the future. But these are likely a good many years off, and we need to act now. Besides, what parent wants his child to have to take medication for obesity if that child can be helped by lifestyle changes—or can avoid the problem altogether with healthy teaching?

If you're looking for a quick fix, you won't find it here. No such thing exists. I offer no gimmicks—no pills for instant weight loss, no "lose weight and get into shape while you sleep" regimens. But you will find straightforward, factual information you can use to help your child.

I've employed these techniques to help effect weight loss in my patients over the years. But I'll be the first to warn you: It will not be easy, and the stakes are high. We must take the attitude of former NASA Flight Director Gene Kranz during the Apollo 13 crisis when he said, "Failure is not an option!"

Each of us is given only one body, and it is a miraculous piece of work. There is quite possibly no more wondrous evidence of God's creative handiwork than the workings of the human body. While we should not worship it, we need to reverence this vehicle for our souls—and those of our children.

—*Robert S. Andersen, M.D., F.A.A.P., F.C.P.*

PART ONE

THE PROBLEM OF CHILDHOOD OBESITY

CHAPTER ONE

A DISTANT THUNDER

I n 1857, Mount St. Helens—in what would later become the state of Washington—settled down after several years of eruptions. For the next 123 years, not a peep was heard from one of the largest volcanoes in the world.

It began to reawaken in March 1980 with daily earthquakes and steam plumes, indicating that a dangerous eruption was possible. Over the next two months, the mountain began to deform, a massive bulge forming on its north face. Scientists suspected a catastrophic explosion was imminent. Local residents were lulled into a false sense of security when the mountain quieted a bit in early May.

On the morning of May 18, Mount St. Helens erupted violently. Pressure blew off the top 1,000 feet of the volcano, with deadly results. Fifty-seven people died that day, most because they failed to heed the warnings of forestry officials.

There was no need for anyone to have been hurt. Some victims had thought officials were being overcautious. Some, like famous area resident Harry Truman, simply refused to leave.

Today, many nations are feeling tremors and seeing steam plumes as the "obesity volcano" rumbles. While the Mount St. Helens blast was unpreventable, we may be able to avoid a worse disaster—an explosion of obesity-related disease.

Many a doctor has noticed increasing numbers of obese children and adults walking through the office door. What physicians have been observing anecdotally for years has now been proven statistically: Obesity rates are steadily rising. Ultimately, this epidemic is likely to contribute to thousands—if not millions—of premature deaths.

How did this happen? Here are some of the reasons. Taken together, they weave quite a tapestry.

REASON #1: LESS EXERCISE

If you're over 35, you may recall childhood summers when you left the house after breakfast and were outside all day, stopping only briefly to use the bathroom and eat a quick lunch. Maybe you'd ride all over town on your bike, play ball with a few friends for hours on end, go to the pool, or collect crayfish at the local stream.

In those days, unorganized neighborhood games of baseball, basketball, street football, kickball, or Capture the Flag took place daily. According to my mom, as a young child I frequently fell asleep at the dinner table—sometimes with my head literally landing in my food—after running around outside all day long. Free of constant parental oversight and organization, kids improvised and played for the fun of it, without pressure.

Today, too many "organized" sports and other activities, especially for younger children, may be robbing kids of the joy of spontaneous games and competition and playing alone. In some places, unsupervised play is simply no longer possible. Legitimate fears of abduction and crime have curtailed much of the freedom children used to have.

In certain urban *and* suburban locations, dangers posed by street gangs force parents to keep their kids inside.

Many parents drive their children everywhere, since it's too far or too dangerous for them to ride their bikes or walk. Fear of litigation has caused many schools and municipalities to remove playground equipment. The bottom line: Children are moving less these days, thus burning fewer calories.

REASON #2: EATING TOO MUCH

"Super-Size it, please!" is the command from the "drive-thru" customer to the fast food employee. What's next, Super-Duper Size? Mega-Super-Duper Size (labeled "Best Value," of course)?

In our culture, we like to feel we're getting our money's worth, and expect things big—especially meal portions. Where else can you get a steak that could feed a small town or a restaurant dessert roughly the size of a toaster?

In France, where people tend to eat a relatively high-fat diet and are avid wine drinkers, the obesity rate is lower—partly because they eat smaller portions at mealtime and do so at a leisurely speed. While I don't advocate the secularist French way of life, the pace and enjoyment of eating there is commendable. Our society's "Texas-size" eating mentality is no doubt affecting many of our children—and not for the better.

We're reaping what we've sown—God's timeless principle. If we can return to modest portion sizes and slower eating, we can begin to have a positive effect on our children's dietary habits. The result: less obesity.

REASON #3: LESS EMPHASIS ON PHYSICAL EDUCATION

As school administrators try to maximize children's academic performance and squeeze precious minutes out of each day, time spent in physical education courses is often reduced. This may not matter for children living in active families, but the rest are missing out on a way to learn how to be physically fit.

Fortunately, some schools are now increasing time spent in P.E.—an encouraging development.

REASON #4: TOO MUCH SCREEN TIME

I admit it: I love my Macintosh laptop computer. I also love watching sports on television. Though I'm not into video games, I've observed patients in my office playing them—and it takes considerable effort to get their attention away from those little electronic marvels.

We live in a digital age, and new avenues of entertainment are only going to proliferate. It's clear, however, that the amount of time spent daily in these pursuits can be directly correlated with childhood obesity rates. Why? Because of inactivity and the powerful effects of food product advertising on TV.

Children's shows are especially laden with food commercials, and I'm not talking about fruits and vegetables. Our marketing gurus are no slouches; they know that a slick ad can seduce us into getting up for a snack halfway through a football game, TV movie, or cartoon. Couple this with the fact that many of the advertised foods and beverages are high in unhealthy fat and sugar (see Chapters 5 and 6) and you've just added another brick to the wall of our epidemic.

Many pediatricians recommend an upper limit of about two hours of TV/video/computer time per day, but a lot of our children greatly exceed that limit. Kids would be much better off with little or no time on the TV, video game system, and computer—and TV is by far the worst of the three because of food advertising. In fact, allowing children to have televisions in their bedrooms is directly tied to increased TV watching and obesity.

REASON #5: LESS EATING AT HOME AS FAMILIES

I can sense the uneasiness as you shift nervously in your seat, preparing for a soapbox lecture. Not to worry. I simply want you to know the facts, and the evidence is clear that families who sit and eat together on a regular basis have lower obesity rates.

This makes perfect sense. More conversation, eating more slowly, consuming fewer meals at fast food establishments, serving normal portion sizes—all would contribute to a smaller total calorie consumption at mealtime. Interestingly, this benefit seems to lessen considerably if the family watches television during the meal.

REASON #6: SUBURBANIZATION

Years ago, people walked to the market daily and bought the food they needed. There was less food around the house; more fresh fruits, vegetables, and whole grains were consumed. An elderly gentleman once told me, "We Americans need to mimic classic Europeans in one thing—we should shop at the market daily and watch TV weekly, instead of the other way around." Sound advice, indeed.

Suburbanization has made this largely impractical. Our kids are walking much less than previous generations. Cars have replaced feet and bicycles as the primary means of transportation.

Are residents of cities and those who live near a town center leaner? The answer isn't simple. When I traveled to London a few years ago, I was taken aback by the apparent lack of obesity. The streets are so crowded that Londoners have to be crazy to drive anywhere, and the "tube" system of underground trains can whisk you anywhere in minutes. Thus, residents walk quite a bit and rely less on automobiles.

While this may account for the seeming lack of obesity in London, it doesn't provide easy answers for everyone. Recent information in the U.S., for example, suggests that obesity rates there may be tied to the affluence of certain areas. The more affluent the area, the less obesity.

This also makes sense. It's more expensive to eat properly; fresh fruits, vegetables, and fish are more costly than canned and processed foods. People with more wealth also tend to be more educated about nutrition and exercise and have easier access to health clubs.

In times past, it was a sign of wealth to be overweight and a mark of poverty to be lean. Today the reverse is true. Poor children are at greatest risk of obesity, and we need to address this fact. Combine that with the trend toward more mechanized transportation and less walking, and you have a direction that needs to be reversed.

REASON #7: FAMILY DISRUPTION

I've observed—though only anecdotally—that obesity seems more common in children of divorced parents than in those whose parents have stayed together. And more children are growing up in families affected by divorce than in the past. This is consistent with the finding that poorer children are more prone to obesity, as divorce places severe financial strains on a family.

It's easy to underestimate the effect of divorce on a child. But the loneliness, depression, and other psychosocial factors that often come with divorce can lead to abnormal eating patterns. Many adults and children eat as a way of soothing themselves; food becomes the one comfort they have in life. Stress may also cause an increase in certain hormones, which can lead to cravings.

It's also logistically much harder for divorced parents to coordinate a healthy eating plan if they have dual custody of a child. The parent who sees a child only on weekends may inadvertently spoil that child by going out regularly to eat more "fun" foods. Many divorced dads lack the knowledge or desire to cook proper meals, and it's often easier to buy fast food.

This is not to say that children of divorce can't overcome weight problems. But it's going to be tougher than usual and requires a high degree of cooperation between parents. With all the challenges facing fractured families, implementing the changes necessary for a child to conquer weight problems can be one very difficult proposition.

REASON #8: FEAR OF EATING DISORDERS

I've seen this often in my practice. Broaching the topic of obesity, however gingerly, elicits looks of fear on some parents' faces. Several have let me know that they're afraid their children might swing back the other way toward anorexia nervosa. This happens mainly in parents of overweight or mildly obese girls.

Gradual reduction toward a normal weight is not a risk factor for anorexia. Though anorexia is possible, the risk is very small. Don't let this concern stop you from helping your child lose weight. If you feel body image distortions are developing, contact your doctor immediately.

REASON #9: FAMILY EXPECTATIONS

Many families have aunts, uncles, grandpas, grandmas, and nannies watch the children while parents work. These caretakers' opinions about a child's weight may differ from the parents' view. "Doctor, he is so skinny!" is a phrase I often hear from grandmothers, despite evidence that the child is growing normally or is even a bit heavy.

I remember a particularly insistent grandmother who, when I said it was normal to see the outline of her six-year-old grandson's ribs, looked at me incredulously. "You can't be serious!" she retorted, obviously wondering if her grandson was under the care of a quack. I was able to dissuade her of that sentiment, but the encounter illustrates a problem doctors often face.

Cultural factors also play a role, causing varied expectations about a child's appearance and food consumption. This can be tough to overcome, and requires a physician to earn the family's complete trust. Clear communication is crucial, too, and any hint of a dictatorial attitude by the doctor may sabotage the process—convincing parents not to comply with recommendations.

REASON #10: MOMENTUM

Children growing up in a home with one or two obese parents are at higher risk for obesity. With more and more parents overweight, more and more children are being raised in these households and imitating parental behavior.

Overweight parents may find it difficult to discuss weight problems with a child, fearing they'll look hypocritical. As with smoking parents who counsel their kids not to take that first puff, this can be tricky.

If you're in this situation, acknowledge that both you and your child have slipped into bad habits—and then correct them together. At the very least, explain the dangers of excess pounds and fully support your child's efforts to lose them.

Are genetics a contributing factor when parent and child are overweight? They can be, but that effect may be overblown. Genes are unlikely to account for the steep increases in obesity rates. Most obese families are the direct result of poor eating and exercise habits developed and passed down through the years. At present we can only control diet and exercise, so it's not helpful to dwell on heredity.

This doesn't mean that genetics have no influence on weight.

Recent studies have described the effect of genetic mutations on appetite control.[1] One example involves an appetite suppression gene. The Melanocortin 4 Receptor (MC4R) works in the hypothalamus of the brain to suppress appetite. The most common mutation, a deficiency of this MC4R gene, occurs in about 6 percent of severely obese children. They have less MC4R, leading to poor appetite control. All these children have markedly increased insulin levels in their blood, which can aid in distinguishing them from other obese children without the mutation.

Future research may identify ways to help these children with medication or gene therapy. (Note: The test for this mutation is not presently available commercially.)

REASON #11: THE ORIGINAL FOOD PYRAMID

Published in 1992 by the U.S. Department of Agriculture, the original Food Pyramid was merely an extension of dietary teaching that began in the 1960s. The premise *seemed* correct: Limit fats and increase grains and vegetables. The problem was that no distinction was made between "good" and "bad" carbohydrates and "good" and "bad" fats.

The lower part of the pyramid consisted of bread, cereal, rice, and pasta; six to eleven servings a day were recommended. As we'll see later in this book, someone could follow this guideline perfectly and be eating poorly. A diet of low-fiber bread, breakfast cereals, rice, and pasta may conform to the pyramid but contains way too many simple, processed carbohydrates. Eating this way can lead to excess weight gain, and it will be of little consolation that the child is eating a "low fat" diet. We need to get back to eating unprocessed grains, high fiber cereals, and whole grain pasta.

Contrary to the impression given by the pyramid, not all foods with higher fat content are bad. Nuts and vegetable oils are perched at the top of the diagram, with no distinction made between very healthy nuts and oils, high in monounsaturated fats, and saturated fats that are unhealthy. The implication is that nuts and oils aren't good for you because they're high in fat. This is simply not true. While they're calorie dense, nuts and certain oils (especially olive oil) should be a significant part of everyone's diet. They're packed with heart-healthy fat—no, that's not a misprint—plus nutrients and calories for energy. They help you feel satisfied and can squelch hunger pangs and cravings, aiding a decrease in snacking.

The pyramid also places legumes (like beans) and fish in the same category as red meats. This is also just plain wrong. Legumes are a fantastic source of protein and fiber without the saturated fat of meat. Certain types of fish, high in omega-3 fatty acids, are very wholesome and should be afforded higher priority than red meat.

As you can see, good intentions often don't accomplish their goals—and may be counterproductive. Recently changes were made to the original pyramid—but the result, in my opinion, is even more confusing than before. I'll have more to say about carbohydrates, fats, and the basics of nutrition later in this book.

These are the main reasons why our kids are becoming heavier and heavier. You may be able to think of a few more.

WHOSE FAULT IS IT, ANYWAY?

Who's responsible for this fix? There's plenty of blame to go around. Government has promoted the misleading Food Pyramid and taken on tasks that belong to parents (feeding their kids, for instance). Physicians have long been lackadaisical in addressing the problem of obesity. Schools have done a poor job by offering less-than-healthy cafeteria fare and allowing soda pop and snack machines on campus. Corporations market junk food to make a buck, supplying products to meet a demand—even if the demand is unhealthy.

Parents bear primary culpability, for they are ultimately account-able for their children's health. In Ephesians 6:4, God does *not* say, "You villages, governments, and schools, bring your children up in the training and admonition of the Lord." No, He addresses fathers.

Eventually children will have to assume care of themselves, but until that time arrives, parents need to be role models, teachers, disci-plinarians, and loving advocates. Once kids reach age 12 or so, they may unwisely reject your recommendations or make things extremely frustrating for you. At some point they must sink or swim on their own. This is why it's so crucial to instill good habits at an early age. Children imitate their parents and learn from them. What example are you setting?

While there may be genetic factors involved in appetite and body type, obesity is ultimately an issue of individual responsibility once a person is over age 12 or so. Remember, we're talking about *obese* chil-dren and adults, not simply *bigger* people with a tendency to be heavy. Some folks may have a genetic tendency toward other types of addic-tions; they must take control of their own destiny to conquer the problem. The same is true of those who are obese.

There's no question that the process is made easier when a parent, friend, or organization supports and provides information to and encourages the person. But the buck stops with the individual.

If obese adults wish to lose weight and get into shape, they have to be the ones to follow through. Deciding what percentage of the problem can be traced to genetics is academic. Many obese people have said to themselves, "Enough is enough," and transformed their lives. They may have languished for years, mired in a terrible diet and inactivity, only to turn things around with knowledge and resolve. They didn't simply "diet," but instituted wholesale lifestyle changes. I know they'd tell you it was well worth the effort.

Children are unable to take on many of these responsibilities, being dependent on their parents. They need you to engage them in these lifestyle changes.

Talk of obesity as a disease is, in my opinion, misguided. In many cases this designation shifts the focus from the responsibility of parents and kids, implying an intrinsic abnormality. But we're talking about exogenous or common obesity, not a hormonal imbalance.

Obesity is really a *symptom* of a larger problem—compulsive overeating, lack of exercise, depression, etc. Like cigarette smoking or excessive drinking, obesity can *cause* disease, but is not a disease in itself. Individuals must be willing to do what it takes to regain their proper shape.

It's human nature to look for someone else to blame when things go awry. Recently, threats of litigation have been aimed at the fast food industry for "causing" obesity. Most of us realize that fast food menus are full of awful things, and wouldn't serve them at home, let alone sell them to others. I believe most ordinary, rational people view these lawsuits as ludicrous, and understand that financial motives may be partially driving those voicing the threats.

Distancing ourselves from the never-ending blame game aids us in squarely facing the problem of obesity. God wants us to take responsibility for ourselves and quit passing the buck. Parents must be accountable for their children just as adults are accountable for themselves.

There are many reasons why obesity rates have risen sharply in the last two decades. Each of the factors listed in this chapter must be evaluated and dealt with if there's to be success in curbing abnormal weight gain.

Parents need to patiently take charge of their children's nutrition and exercise routines. It won't be easy, and you may have failed in the past. But be persistent and get help from your friends, family, pastor, and doctor.

In a later section, I'll outline a program for helping your child stay slim and fit—or to begin overcoming obesity and unfitness. In the meantime, let's find out why your efforts to raise fit kids could be a matter of life and death.

CHAPTER TWO

THE APPROACHING TSUNAMI

What will happen if the childhood obesity epidemic isn't dealt with decisively?

Think back to December 2004, when a tsunami devastated south Asia, killing hundreds of thousands of people.

A tsunami, or tidal wave, travels silently under the surface of the ocean, sometimes for hundreds of miles, before crashing onto land and wreaking havoc. The powerful earthquake that set the 2004 tsunami in motion was detectable; yet systems were not in place to conclusively predict the tsunami and warn the susceptible areas. Thus, some of the waves moved stealthily for hours and hundreds of miles before raising their ugly heads onto the beaches.

Similarly, obesity is traveling quietly through many parts of the world. It will manifest itself in the years to come with an increase in serious medical complications.

This metaphor is sound. While the Asian tsunami was a tragedy of epic proportions, ultimately many more lives will end prematurely due to the complications of obesity than were lost in December 2004—unless we can reverse the course of the epidemic.

WHAT'S THE PROBLEM?

What's so bad about having more fat cells? Why does obesity breed life-threatening difficulties?

The answer appears to point toward chronic, low-grade inflammation. An evolving focus of research in this area involves chemicals known as cytokines. We know cytokines cause inflammation, and fat cells produce them. Evidence of this inflammation in the fat cells of obese children recently was presented in a study from Italy.[1] The more fat cells, the higher the risk of inflammation; the more inflammation, the greater the chance of serious conditions occurring.

Regardless of the cause, obesity is a dangerous condition and a slow killer. Some of the problems it produces can appear in childhood, but generally they take decades to develop.

Here are some of the conditions for which obesity is a risk factor.

CONDITION #1: HYPERTENSION

High blood pressure—hypertension—is a serious risk factor for kidney disease, heart attack, and stroke. Because there are usually no symptoms, many people go undiagnosed and damage is done gradually. Hypertension is truly a "silent killer."

My 16-year-old patient, J.J., and his parents were a bit taken aback when I told them his blood pressure was elevated. His reading of 142/82 was much too high. Subsequent measurements confirmed the elevation. Realizing the dangers of hypertension, J.J. and his parents decided to act aggressively to solve the problem.

First and foremost, he needed to lose weight—even though he was a lineman on the football team. At 72.5 inches tall and 204.5 pounds, he had a body mass index (BMI; see Chapter 8) of 27.35—definitely high for his age. After counseling, he began to run regularly with his dad and sister and ate more slowly. He also chose healthier fare, cutting out some of the snacks and junk food he'd been eating regularly.

Four months later, he was down to 181 pounds. His BMI was 24.2, his blood pressure 130/78. At this writing, J.J. realizes he isn't out of the woods; his blood pressure is still too high. But he's motivated to keep improving his fitness so that he's less likely to need blood pressure medication—and less likely to develop heart disease in the future.

CONDITION #2: CORONARY ARTERY DISEASE

Blockage of the arteries that supply blood to the muscles of the heart is much more common in obese individuals than in those of normal weight.

A study in the medical journal *Endocrinology*, published in 2003, reviewed the relationship between increased fat cells and damage to blood vessels.[2] It appears that damage to the lining of our arteries may take place due to the effects of certain chemicals and cells, such as cytokines and macrophages. These mediators of the inflammatory response are increased in the obese. It's very likely that this process begins early in overweight kids; in its final stages, a heart attack can result.

The leading cause of death in our society is heart disease. If we don't deal with the problem of obesity, its incidence will continue to rise in the years to come.

CONDITION #3: TYPE 2 DIABETES

This is a big one. The risk of developing this kind of diabetes rises greatly in overweight people.

The medical community used to think that when a child developed diabetes, it was always type 1—a "burning out" of the insulin-producing cells in the pancreas, causing permanent insulin deficiency. Now we're seeing more and more children with type 2 diabetes—a decrease in insulin production accompanied by insulin resistance. In other words, the pancreas produces less insulin, and what it does make is not as efficient in doing its job.

I don't remember seeing a case of type 2 diabetes in a child during the first 14 years of my pediatric practice. But I've seen several in just the past 4. In one case, the mom looked at me, stunned, when she learned her son had the same kind of diabetes as his grandmother. "I thought that only happened in old people," she said in disbelief. The diagnosis was not entirely surprising, since the whole family was overweight.

Evidence of glucose intolerance—an early sign of type 2 diabetes—may be present in up to one-quarter of obese children.[3] Complications of uncontrolled diabetes include heart disease, kidney disease, retinal damage, damage to nerves and blood vessels resulting in decreased sensation and impotence, and lipid problems (see Condition #4).

Diabetes is especially serious in children. Having so much longer to live, they have more time for complications to develop. Many adolescents diagnosed with type 2 diabetes in the next few years may suffer kidney failure in 20, 30, or 40 years. This will place an enormous strain on our health care system as well as on the individuals and families involved.

CONDITION #4: LIPID PROBLEMS

High triglyceride levels, high "bad" cholesterol (low-density lipoprotein, or LDL) or low "good" cholesterol (high-density lipoprotein, or HDL) levels are all more common in the overweight person. Combined with inflammation, lipid abnormalities lead to coronary heart disease and may also be linked to Alzheimer's disease and strokes.

Exercise is one way to lower LDL and triglycerides and raise HDL. Proper eating habits are another.

Some thin people have this problem, too, genetically transmitted from their parents. If wholesome eating, regular exercise, and weight loss don't resolve lipid abnormalities, "statin" medicines may be prescribed to lower LDL and raise HDL levels.

CONDITION #5: STROKE

Linked to hypertension and lipid abnormalities, stroke risk increases in an obese person. A stroke can result from bleeding into the brain or from a blockage in one of the arteries there.

The result is typically the death of significant areas of the brain, often with severe and permanent disabilities. Most people do not need to be reminded of the potentially devastating effects of a stroke.

CONDITION #6: GALL BLADDER DISEASE

While not usually fatal, this can cause extreme pain and can lead to potentially serious complications. Surgery is often required to treat the problem, and surgery is always more difficult and risky in obese individuals.

CONDITION #7: OSTEOARTHRITIS

Because of extra stress on weight-bearing joints, osteoarthritis is more common in the obese. In a cruel cycle, once arthritis develops, movement becomes increasingly painful—making weight loss and fitness harder to achieve.

CONDITION #8: CANCER

Breast, colon, endometrial, and prostate cancer rates may be elevated in the obese; surveillance research is ongoing.

This elevated rate may be due to the increased inflammation mentioned earlier. Also, it's more difficult for doctors to detect growths by examining an overweight patient; they can't feel things as well through layers of fatty tissue, which could delay diagnosis of certain types of malignancies. In addition, the weight loss that can be a sign of cancer is not as noticeable in an overweight person as it is in a lean one.

CONDITION #9: SLEEP APNEA

Caused by a blockage in the breathing passages of the nose and throat, this condition can cause sleep problems and extreme fatigue. In severe cases, it also can lead to heart failure due to chronic lack of oxygen at night. This blockage occurs, in part, due to fat buildup in these areas.

CONDITION #10: FATTY LIVER DISEASE

Just as fat accumulates in other areas of the body, it can build up in the liver. Certain obese children seem prone to store an unusually high amount of fat in their livers. In the worst cases, cirrhosis can result— as it can in a person who drinks alcohol heavily. This may cause liver failure.

Liver transplants have been necessary for these children, all because of obesity! Unless it's too late, weight loss is the only remedy.

CONDITION #11: ASTHMA

Asthma rates are higher in obese kids than in other kids. Children with asthma have inflamed airways, and control of this inflammation is the hallmark of asthma treatment. Since obese children have more inflammation in their bodies, it's no surprise that asthma can be a complicating condition.

It's a challenge to treat very overweight children who have asthma, since they're often short of breath due to their obesity. This makes it more difficult to assess how many of their symptoms are due to asthma—and how many to obesity.

CONDITION #12: INCREASED DEATH RATE FROM ALL CAUSES

Any disease process becomes potentially more serious in an overweight patient, leading to higher rates of mortality. In other words, obesity can make practically any illness more dangerous.

CONDITION #13: PSYCHOLOGICAL PROBLEMS

Many overweight kids are wonderfully happy and well adjusted. But evidence shows that obese children experience more social isolation and peer discrimination than other children do.

Obese girls have moderately higher rates of clinical depression compared to their slimmer peers.[4] Boys seem less susceptible to depressive symptoms, but both sexes suffer higher rates of social marginalization.[5] There's no question that obese kids are stigmatized and face discrimination when it comes to friendships.

Two studies—one in 1961 and the other conducted recently for comparison—revealed the disadvantage obese children suffer in peer relationships.[6] When kids were shown pictures of various children and asked how much they'd like each one, obese kids were almost always picked last as preferred friends. Even more worrisome: The good opinion of lean children's pictures and the bad opinion of obese children's *increased* in the last 40 years. The bottom line: Obese kids are experiencing even more discrimination than before.

In the world of kids, weight-based teasing is pervasive. It breaks my heart to hear overweight children tell me they're ridiculed at school. Worse, needling and unconstructive criticism occur at home, too. This treatment can lead to a poor self-image, depression, and even suicidal thoughts.[7]

One girl tearfully told me that no one liked her "because I am fat." My heart ached for her; it was all I could do to keep the tears from welling up in my own eyes. Life is tough enough without having to deal with the rejection posed by the stigma of obesity.

If your child suffers that kind of rejection, what can you do? The aforementioned study that showed how both sexes are socially marginalized for being obese also showed that these kids benefit from sports participation, club involvement, and less television viewing. In addition, parents need to demonstrate unconditional love to all their kids—especially those who struggle with weight problems. Siblings should be taught to be sensitive and supportive, too.

That was the case with a patient of mine. Steve was an 11-year-old who saw me for an exam one summer. After asking to meet with me separately before the checkup, his mom told me that Steve had been sneaking food for several years. When she asked him about it, he would deny it. Now he was overweight—and seemed not to care. She was frustrated—and fearful that her husband would berate Steve if he knew of the boy's furtive eating. Mom explained that even though

Dad loved his son, he was harshly critical whenever the boy didn't perform up to standards.

Clearly there was more to Steve's behavior than a simple lack of appetite control. This was a case of a child feeling depressed due to excessive censure by a well-meaning but overly critical parent.

After I encouraged her, Mom and Dad met with their pastor for counseling. Soon Mom told her husband about Steve's eating habits.

I saw Steve and his mother a few months later. Things seemed better, though the boy hadn't lost any weight. Mom said that Dad was still strict, but much more gracious and patient with his son.

About a year after I first saw them, they were back. Steve seemed much happier. He'd maintained his weight but had grown 2.5 inches.

Here's the moral of the story for us parents: While we need to set clear limits and discipline decisively when needed, it must always be in a spirit of love and grace. Kids—including obese ones—desperately need to know of God's unconditional love for them. No better foundation exists for a healthy self-image than to know the Creator of the universe loves and values you.

HIGHER GROUND

As we see more obese children become obese adults, we'll see a rise in the conditions I've just described. The tsunami is headed our way. Are we resourceful enough to get out of its path—and not make it worse?

You can see how important this is to the health of our children, our society, and the world. I think you're ready for the next step—understanding the dietary recommendations and lifestyle changes needed to accomplish the goal of safe, lasting weight loss and physical fitness. That's why I'm enrolling you in Physiology 101.

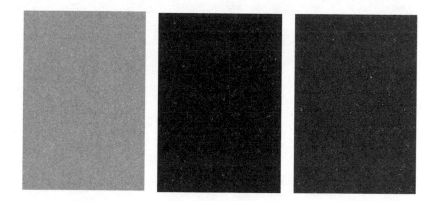

PART TWO

PHYSIOLOGY 101

CHAPTER THREE

THE BASICS OF METABOLISM

E ver heard someone say, "He's lean because he has a good metabolism"?

What does that mean? Is a "good metabolism" something you can develop, or are we simply born a certain way?

The answer isn't so obvious: It's both.

I remember how my dad used to say, in response to my prodigious intake of food during adolescence, "Have you got a hollow leg?" The combination of rapid growth and constant physical activity revved up my metabolism, making increased calorie intake necessary.

Like my young self, most children have pretty active engines. How many times I've heard from moms, "He doesn't stop from sunup to sundown!" Some kids have a lower or higher genetic metabolism, but the differences are not all that great. Intake and activity are the keys.

And yes—I'm sorry to report that my hollow leg has now filled in.

DRIVING YOUR BMR

"Metabolism" is simply the process by which living creatures take food and turn it into energy for growth, tissue repair, internal heat to stay warm, fuel for activities, etc. The term Basal Metabolic Rate (BMR) represents a person's inherent metabolic rate—his or her "metabolism," if you will.

BMR represents the number of calories the body burns per hour when it is stationary, is relaxed, is well rested, has a normal temperature, is in a normal thermal environment, and hasn't eaten in twelve hours or exercised for at least one hour. Stated another way, BMR is the energy your body needs to survive when you're acting like a total couch potato.

To account for size differences, BMR usually is expressed as it relates to the surface area of the person—calories burned per hour per square meter of surface area. Men have a slightly higher BMR than women, and everyone's BMR slowly diminishes with age. That's how those hollow legs fill up.

Some people are born with a slower BMR than others. If all other factors (gender, size, exercise, sleep, emotional stress, and calorie intake) are equal, and there are no differences in thermal stress (for example, living in San Diego instead of Alaska in January), then the person with the slower BMR will weigh more.

The good news is that BMR is a relatively small factor in determining a person's ultimate weight, and can be increased. Since muscle burns calories even at rest, building muscle mass through strength training is a simple way to elevate BMR.

Unfortunately, having a "slow metabolism" is frequently used as an excuse for obesity when the person or family lacks the motivation or knowledge to deal with the problem.

YOUR TDEE TODAY

As important as BMR may be, more crucial to weight control is a person's Total Daily Energy Expenditure (TDEE). TDEE is the number of calories a person burns in a day—your BMR plus all the other things you do including exercise, the "work" of eating, digesting food, keeping warm on a cold day, thinking, etc. Remember, BMR is the energy you use just to stay alive; TDEE includes everything else.

When it comes to weight loss, TDEE is the key. It needs to be higher than calorie intake if you're going to lose weight. The best way to increase your TDEE is to augment your daily physical activities— taking the stairs instead of elevators, exercising regularly, walking instead of driving, not sitting in front of the television too much, etc.

There are two sides to the metabolism equation. On one side is the amount of food we take in each day; on the other side is the TDEE.

Daily Caloric Intake   *TDEE (BMR + all other*
energy expenditures)

How the above equation balances determines what's happening with our body weight. If the left side is greater, we'll be gaining weight. If the right side is greater, we'll be losing it. This is a very simplistic schema, but helpful for our purposes.

I got a firsthand lesson in the power of this energy equation when I was a resident doctor in training. On-call doctors were often at the hospital for 36 hours at a time. These could be lonely stretches, late at night away from home and family. Loneliness and boredom can lead to excessive food intake—for adults as well as children.

My second year of training was particularly grueling. For several months of that year, I spent every third night at the hospital. Since my colleagues and I were often up much of the night, we hung out in the cafeteria. Unfortunately for us, they served food 24/7. Worse yet, food was free to resident doctors.

I usually weigh about 165 pounds (or 12 stone, in British parlance). But that year I gained around 10 pounds—simply by eating extra food every third night and not getting outside as much as usual. I'll never forget that summer, when I traveled home for a vacation and saw my wonderful late grandfather Sverre Andersen. He said with a smile as he hugged me, "Boy, are you fat!"

I laughed about it then, and still do now. But it impressed on me the power of a few extra calories per day over a period of time. Take-home message: Unnecessary calories here and there can make a big difference in the long run.

THE IMPORTANCE OF BEING PATIENT

Often people get into trouble when they try to change drastically only one side of the equation—or change both sides too much, too soon.

Cutting back dramatically on food intake through fasting or "crash" dieting can fool the body into thinking it's starving. This reflexively lowers the BMR—the result of a built-in survival mechanism. In essence your body says, "Hey, we're starving here! Time to slow this old crate down to conserve energy!"

This is why it's crucial to *gradually* reduce caloric intake while *gradually* increasing TDEE—thus allowing your body to adjust. You don't want to throw the frog into the boiling water, so to speak; you want to start cool and ratchet the heat up steadily so he doesn't notice. Simply walking 30 minutes a day is enough to nudge people toward gradual weight loss by increasing TDEE slightly.

On the other side of the equation, it's estimated that in adults, decreasing intake by just 200 calories per day can result in a 20-pound weight loss in one year. Note that this could be accomplished by eliminating one 16-ounce serving of regular soda pop per day. The concept is the same for children.

One of my patients, Charlie, found out how true this is. Having had no prior health problems and a history of being lean, he came in for a routine checkup when he was 13. His weight had ballooned from 115 pounds to 145 in one year. At 67 inches tall, he had a body mass index of 22.7—above the 85th percentile.

I found in talking to his mom that the reason was simple: Charlie had way too much sugar in his diet. By her calculation he sometimes consumed up to 120 grams of sugar at lunch alone! Soda pop was a big offender.

Mom and Charlie simply cut out the excess sugar and determined to eat better foods. Within one year, without any change in his exercise habits, Charlie was down to 125 pounds. His BMI was now a very healthy 18.5. He continues to grow normally and maintain a healthy weight, up to 135 pounds and 71 inches tall.

This should be an encouragement to you if you're thinking there's no way you can get your child to lose weight. You don't have to do anything dramatic. Cut back on excess calories, especially those with little or no nutritional benefit, and begin to elevate your child's TDEE. You'll be starting him or her down the road to fitness.

Remember: *Any attempt to lose weight by focusing on only one side of the equation is less likely to bring success.* If you only cut back on calories, you'll eventually lose weight—but you won't be more fit. Similarly, exercising without improving your diet will help—but won't bring optimal health. You must improve both sides of the equation!

This concept is worth cementing in your mind as you seek to help yourself and your child. So is the one you'll learn in the next chapter—about the unseen but unmistakable influence of a well-known hormone.

CHAPTER FOUR

INSULIN—FRIEND *AND* FOE?

Of all the substances in the body, the hormone called insulin may have the most important effect on a person's weight. Since insulin's discovery in 1922, most people in our society have heard of its influence on blood sugar. But it has a profound effect on fat and protein metabolism, too.

Understanding how this works will help you grasp why I'm going to recommend certain dietary changes. It will also explain why, despite years of preaching the well-intentioned "food pyramid" to children, they continue to put on excess weight.

HOW IT WORKS

The beta cells of the pancreas produce insulin, and secrete it directly into the bloodstream when needed—especially when blood sugar (glucose) surges, as it does shortly after a high-carbohydrate meal. The amount of insulin produced is finely tuned to the sugar load that needs to be metabolized, so glucose levels normally stay in a narrow range. To a lesser degree, protein intake also stimulates insulin secretion, but fat digestion results in little or no insulin being produced.

Insulin most profoundly affects muscle, fat, and liver cells. It circulates in the bloodstream for about 10 to 15 minutes unless it binds to a cell's insulin receptor. Several important things happen when that connection takes place:

1. Blood glucose and amino acids enter the cell for use. Thus, a lack of insulin means glucose has a hard time getting into the cell, resulting in a high blood sugar level.

If the blood glucose level keeps rising, it will eventually exceed the kidneys' ability to hold on to it (typically at levels over 180, normal being 70-110). When this happens, glucose spills into the urine, pulling water along with it, and we see some classic symptoms of diabetes—excessive urination and thirst.

Eventually, in type 1 diabetes, dehydration and weight loss result. Because cells are not getting the energy they need from glucose, the body begins to starve—not a good thing. With type 2 diabetes, insulin is still produced, but at lower levels; cells begin to resist insulin's actions. The result is an insidious rise in blood glucose levels that slowly damage the body. As you can see, adequate amounts of insulin are absolutely crucial to our health.

2. In the liver, insulin causes glucose to be stored as a quick-release, energy-storing compound called glycogen. Any glucose the liver can't handle is packaged as fatty acids, the building blocks of fat, which eventually are stored as fat. This is why excessive insulin levels and obesity can lead to fatty liver disease.

3. Insulin causes the sparing of fat—that is, it inhibits fat breakdown. Dr. Robert Atkins capitalized on this fact in his famous diet. When a person on this regimen severely cuts back on carbohydrate intake, his insulin secretion falls and the body begins to burn fat for

energy instead of storing it. (I'll have more to say about the Atkins Diet in Chapter 6.)

4. Insulin slows the breakdown of protein for energy. It also increases protein production.

This simple summary of insulin metabolism doesn't tell the whole story, of course. The subtle effects of this tiny protein and the complexity of its interactions with other hormones are staggering and beyond the scope of this book. The intricacies of insulin are but another evidence that we're "fearfully and wonderfully made" (Psalm 139:14).

For now, it's enough to say that insulin plays a crucial role in helping the body metabolize blood sugar, to spare fat and protein, and to build fat and protein stores. Insulin is absolutely vital for good health—but like water or fire, too much of it can be dangerous. Elevated insulin levels cause weight gain and hunger. A poor diet is usually their cause, and can be corrected.

JOE'S STORY

One sign of chronically increased insulin levels (what we doctor types call "hyperinsulinism") may be a skin condition called *acanthosis nigricans.* This thickening and darkening of the skin, most commonly around the neck and armpits, makes even the cleanest child look as if she's been playing in the dirt and forgot to use soap at bath time.

I say this *may* be a sign of hyperinsulinism because it's not certain whether the condition is due to excess weight or is directly connected to increased insulin levels. Regardless, when a doctor sees this in an overweight child, evaluation is necessary for hyperinsulinism and early type 2 diabetes.

One such patient of mine, Joe, is a delightful boy with a great sense of humor. When I first saw him, he'd been healthy overall; but I was concerned because his father was quite obese and Joe was gaining weight too quickly as he grew.

Despite counseling, Joe continued to get bigger. By age 13, his body mass index was 24.74, just under the 95th percentile. I also noticed mild *acanthosis nigricans* when I examined his neck.

Joe, his mom, and I discussed the findings. I recommended testing him for early type 2 diabetes, and that he embark on a long-term strategy for weight optimization. Fortunately, his lab tests came back normal.

Still, Joe responded like a champion to my re-emphasized recommendations. Four months later, he'd grown nearly an inch and lost 14 pounds. His BMI was now 21.5, less than the 85th percentile. Better still, his *acanthosis* was lessening.

When I asked him what he thought was his key to success, he smiled. Shrugging his shoulders as if to indicate it was no big deal, he said, "I am eating better and I have been going outside more to play basketball."

He added that he didn't feel hungry—a vital factor in weight loss strategies. I could tell Joe was going to do well. It was clear that he was motivated and happy with his new, fitter self.

THE LONG-TERM ANSWER

It won't surprise you if I say that most kids in our society eat too much. Combine this excessive intake with the kind of food consumed, and you have a recipe for disaster. A bowl of sugary cereal in the morning; a greasy cheeseburger with fries, a soft drink, and dessert for lunch; snacks after school; pizza for dinner; ice cream before bedtime; you get the picture.

When children or adults consume more than their bodies need—especially too many simple, processed carbohydrates—their bodies secrete too much insulin into their bloodstreams, with harmful effects. Fat is stored and not used for energy, resulting in obesity.

Many severely obese people enter a chronic state of increased insulin levels—hyperinsulinism. In essence, they're in a state of perpetual fat-building, which is extremely hard to end. This puts them at high risk for type 2 diabetes.

Eventually, a person in this state will find his pancreas has tired out. His body's cells will begin resisting the excess insulin, which will not work as well as it used to. The result: increasing blood glucose levels, the first sign of diabetes.

Research is underway to see if there's a way to break this cycle with medication. Some medicines used for type 2 diabetes help in the short-term treatment of hyperinsulinism with insulin resistance. But the long-term answer is correcting diet and increasing exercise.

If I've done my job, you now have a basic understanding of human metabolic physiology. Congratulations!

But there's one more course at No-Gimmick University in which I'd like to enroll you: Nutrition 101. When it comes to weight control, this is one class you can't afford to skip.

PART THREE

NUTRITION 101

CHAPTER FIVE

THE CARB CONTROVERSY

Ah, the diet wars—never a dull moment! You read about a new weight loss strategy one day and are told something different by your doctor the next—only to be finally "set straight" by your mother-in-law.

For instance, conventional wisdom says fatty foods make you fat and cause high cholesterol, which is linked with heart disease. So how is it that your neighbor is eating a higher-fat diet, losing weight, and his cholesterol is dropping? What's going on?

Is fat a villain or a hero? What about carbohydrates? Some say eat them, others say no. Are you ready to throw up your hands in disgust and frustration?

Don't.

Medical knowledge evolves slowly. It's often two steps forward, one back—and frustrating at times to professional and lay folks alike. Generally, when you hear such disparate claims and "solid" studies on both sides of an issue, the truth lies somewhere in the middle.

On the current diet battlefield, we see one camp castigating carbs, the other fats. In the next two chapters we'll look at both substances—and see that both are necessary components of the human diet. But all fats are not the same, and neither are all carbohydrates. Knowing the differences can make it a lot easier to raise fit kids.

CRASH COURSE ON CARBS

There are three sources of energy in the human diet: carbohydrates, fat, and protein. Plant foods are the major source of carbohydrates.

All carbohydrates eventually break down into one of three sugars—glucose, fructose, or galactose. The body digests fructose and galactose quickly, producing glucose; so for all practical purposes, glucose is the main actor on the carbohydrate metabolism stage.

Glucose is quickly absorbed into the bloodstream, and must be dealt with. As we saw in the previous chapter, the body responds to increases in blood sugar by producing insulin—which is responsible for handling glucose in the bloodstream and keeping it within certain tight parameters. The effect of insulin completes the digestive process of carbohydrates—by driving glucose into cells to be used for energy or storage.

The body can call upon these stored compounds for energy as needed. Each gram of carbohydrate produces four calories of energy, the same as protein. In contrast, fat has nine calories of energy per gram.

Most children in our society receive 50 to 60 percent of their calories per day from carbohydrates. Carb-rich foods like vegetables, fruits, and whole grains are a critical part of a child's diet. Besides delivering energy for growing kids, they contribute fiber, antioxidants, phytonutrients, vitamins, and minerals. They also prevent the breakdown of body proteins.

In a state of starvation, once carbohydrate and fat reserves are depleted, the body begins to use protein for energy—resulting in the wasting of muscle. That's why authors of early low-carb diets urged adequate intake of fat and protein so as not to cause protein breakdown. Several popular diets—including Atkins, South Beach, and the Zone—all look to reducing carbohydrate intake in order to burn fat and lose weight without muscle wasting.

A portly friend of mine in medical school tried what was then called a "protein sparing fast." He ate virtually nothing but protein for a month, supplemented by vitamins and electrolytes. Though he lost a considerable amount of weight, he looked haggard and said he felt terrible. He was constantly hungry.

Having realized this was no way to live, he gave up—and binged on carbohydrates until he gained back his extra weight. Needless to say, this was not a healthy, sensible thing to do. He learned a valuable lesson: There are no shortcuts to healthy weight loss.

THE GLYCEMIC INDEX

Not all carbohydrates are created equal. Some break down quickly to glucose, flooding the bloodstream, causing larger amounts of insulin to be needed quickly. Others take longer to be digested, causing more gradual releases of glucose and insulin.

Processed carbohydrates like refined sugar, white rice, white bread, and crackers—the things most kids in our society eat—have had much of the fiber removed and fall into the former category. Most unprocessed carbohydrates—like whole-grain bread or a piece of fresh broccoli—fall into the latter. Forget what you may have learned about "starches," "simple sugars," and "complex sugars"; looking at carbohydrate metabolism in terms of glucose and insulin release is where the rubber meets the road.

In fact, there's a way to measure this phenomenon and how it affects weight control. It's called the glycemic index—"GI" for short (see Appendix A). The glycemic index of a certain food is a number that tells you about the carbohydrates in that food and how quickly they break down into glucose and enter the bloodstream. All foods are compared to the "gold standard" carbohydrate—glucose, which is assigned a GI of 100.

A food's glycemic index is determined by feeding a defined amount of that food to a person who's been fasting, and then monitoring his or her blood glucose. After several of those measurements, each result is plotted on a graph; the area under the curve determines the GI value.

For example, a Golden Delicious apple has a GI of 39; it produces glucose in the bloodstream at 39 percent of the level of a pure glucose "meal." The lower the GI value, the lower and more gradual the glucose surge. Since the body has a harder time digesting carbohydrates with lower GI scores, they digest more slowly—creating smaller glucose loads and lower insulin levels.

THE GLYCEMIC LOAD

The glycemic index doesn't take into account the *amount* of the carbohydrate in a food—only how it affects the body in comparison with pure glucose. The glycemic load, or GL, (see Appendix A) takes a food's GI and multiplies it by the number of carbohydrate grams to help you determine how much that serving will cause your blood glucose and insulin to surge.

When I talk about a glucose surge, I don't mean that your blood glucose level swings wildly in and out of the normal range. I'm saying that the amount of insulin needed to keep glucose levels in the normal range goes up substantially.

Let's say the aforementioned apple has a GI of 39 and a GL of 5.7. Apple juice, in contrast, has a GI of 40—nearly identical to the apple—but a GL of 10.6. Your child would be getting almost twice the glycemic load after drinking a serving of apple juice than she would by eating a Golden Delicious apple. Having the apple instead of the juice would reduce the amount of insulin the body has to secrete in order to handle that glucose load—in addition to being far healthier due to the fiber and phytonutrients.

WHAT DIFFERENCE DOES IT MAKE?

Avoiding spikes and drops in insulin may help to curb the cravings and hunger swings common in some children. This is a fact you can use *now* to start helping your child conquer overeating.

A study published in 2003[1] showed that meals with lower GI values cause less extreme glucose and insulin responses than higher-GI meals do. Those fed the lower GI foods felt satisfied longer, too. They ate the same number of calories as the higher GI group, but researchers hope that increased satiety will lead to reduced snacking. Even if it doesn't, the lower insulin levels sparked by lower-GI meals mean less fat produced and not burned.

How can you use GI and GL to your advantage? We'll look at that question in greater detail in later chapters, but here are just two principles to get you started.

1. More thorough cooking will increase the GI of many foods. Pasta, for instance, should be cooked so that it's firm, not mushy. This results in the pasta having a slightly lower GI than overcooked pasta. It has the same number of calories, but will result in a lower insulin surge.

2. The more fat or fiber in a food, the lower the GI. Some nuts and seeds, for example, are high in healthy fat and have low GI values. Whole grain bread has lower GI and GL values than processed breads from which the fiber has been removed.

Some people dismiss the practical value of the GI, saying we seldom eat foods in isolation—and that mixing foods changes the overall

GI, rendering it meaningless. But children often eat a food by itself—pretzels, crackers, cookies, or bread, for instance. Others feel that only a food's caloric content counts. But even though calories are very important, foods that don't cause insulin surges may decrease cravings and feelings of hunger—thus making your efforts to raise fit kids more likely to succeed.

The bottom line: Avoid as many high-GI and high-GL foods as possible. It's not the only answer, but it will play a vital role in helping your child gain control of his or her appetite.

A quick glance at the GI and GL lists (see Appendix A) will reveal some commonly eaten foods you'll want to cut back on. You'll also find some foods with lower GI and GL values that will increase the amount of fiber your child gets, as well as causing fewer insulin spikes.

ALEXA'S STORY

One young lady I see in my practice is a beautiful example of these principles in action. Alexa is 15. She loves to play soccer, hang out at the mall, and talk on the phone with friends. She has a wonderful, supportive family, a bubbly personality, and enthusiasm for golf.

By the time Alexa was 13, her weight had reached the 90th percentile—even though her height was at the 25th. The change had been very gradual, so her parents were caught by surprise. Soon Alexa and her folks realized there was a problem.

As we talked, it became apparent that she'd slipped into some rather unhealthy eating habits. Despite an active lifestyle and plenty of exercise, her diet was downright awful. She'd become a soda pop and Gatorade junkie. Like many children, she'd started drinking Gatorade after soccer practice and while playing golf. Since she so enjoyed the taste, she continued to do so at home. She'd also developed a penchant for snacks, sweets, and bread.

My examination confirmed that Alexa was very healthy. She showed no signs of any physical problem causing her weight gain. Yet at 134 pounds and 60 inches tall, she had a body mass index of 26.2—slightly higher than the 95th percentile, and officially obese.

Alexa and her family were willing to make the changes necessary for success. Simple counseling and encouragement were enough, partly because Alexa and her parents quickly realized the cause of her obesity.

We stopped the soda pop, Gatorade, and most sweets and snacks. Whole grain breads replaced white bread. The entire family instituted a more wholesome diet, and she continued to stay active.

In one year Alexa lost 10 pounds and grew another three-quarters of an inch. Her BMI was now 23.6, just above the 85th percentile. The improvement continued between ages 14 and 15; she grew another half inch while her weight stayed the same, dropping her BMI to just below the 85th percentile. Today Alexa says she has more energy, has fewer headaches and drowsy spells, and wants to continue to eat well and "stay in shape."

THE RIGHT STUFF

So here's the straight story on carbs: Children need them, and especially the fiber and nutrients contained in fruits, vegetables, legumes, and whole grains. They absolutely do *not* need the junk carbohydrates—refined sugar being most notorious among them—with high glycemic loads that lead to high insulin levels that can contribute to obesity.

Any no-gimmick program to lose weight and keep it off should include a diligent effort to substantially reduce high-GI foods. It's not as simple as avoiding or not avoiding carbs. Feed your children the *right* carbohydrates, with higher fiber content and a lower GI, and you'll go a long way toward fitness.

CHAPTER SIX

THE FATS OF LIFE

L ike carbohydrates, fat is a vital part of a child's diet. Because it's the densest kind of food energy, it's ideal for a growing youngster.

Most children in the U.S. consume 30 to 40 percent of their calories in the form of fat. Some low-carb diets recommend even more. Most researchers concerned with heart health, however, suggest getting about 30 percent of total calories from fat.

Fat has its downside, of course. But it has its benefits, too. One is its protein-sparing action. In other words, when you have enough fat around for energy, your body won't use its own muscle protein for that purpose.

In this chapter, we'll look at how fats—and which types of fats—fit into the diet of a healthy child.

FAT: A PRACTICAL APPROACH

Knowing how much fat a typical child eats is fine, but is it going to help you plan your meals? Have you ever calculated—or even thought about calculating—what percentages of carbohydrate, fat, and protein your child consumes? Would you even have a clue about how to start? Is this really a practical way to guide you on what to feed your children?

I believe that for the vast majority of parents, the answer to those questions is a resounding "No." It might be nice to have a dietitian or nutritionist standing next to you in the kitchen each time you prepare a meal, but I doubt this will happen anytime soon. We need to come up with a more pragmatic way.

As you'll hear more than once in this book, I believe that if children are offered a variety of foods, their bodies will guide them to eat the correct balance of protein, carbohydrates, and fat. The key is offering them a *wholesome* variety.

When it comes to fat intake, as with carbohydrates, of utmost importance is what *kind* your child consumes. I want you to feed your child healthier, monounsaturated fat and fat sources high in omega-3, a heart-healthy nutrient. Offer fewer portions of less healthy saturated animal fat. Try to eliminate unhealthy trans fat—as found in cookies, pastries, French fries, and the like.

Since most of us are conditioned to eat more of the latter and little of the former, this will take some effort on your part. If you have a newborn or a very young child, this is your opportunity to teach him correct eating habits; he'll come to think of this as the normal way to eat. For older children, who may have been eating too much fat or the wrong kind of fat for years, it's a tougher transition. It's harder to stop a train once it has a full head of steam—but it *can* be stopped.

FAT, MILK, AND KIDS

One staple in the diets of most young children is milk. But what kind of milk do they need? Should you be concerned about its fat content?

During the first two years after birth, proper development of a child's brain depends in part on the intake of "essential" fatty acids.

The body can't make these; they must be obtained through food, and are found only in dietary fat. That's why fat restriction must be undertaken with great care in this age range. If a young child doesn't eat enough essential fatty acids, developmental disadvantages can result.

In the past few years, infant formulas have been fortified with these nutrients—and there are now supplements available for nursing moms. Fortunately for brain growth, it's rare for most children in our society to consume too little fat.

For years pediatricians have recommended that children drink whole (full fat) milk from at least age one to age two, as the brain develops. This is still standard dogma in most pediatric circles. Now that we're seeing such a rise in obesity, though, some are asking if this is truly necessary—especially in a society with access to a large variety of quality foods. Do children really *need* to drink whole milk instead of 2 percent?

A large study from Finland[1] compared children of this age who were on lower-saturated-fat and higher-saturated-fat diets. The researchers gave skim milk to the study group children after 12 months of age and used 2 percent milk for the control group. What did they find? No discernable differences in developmental outcomes or growth were seen between the two groups—but significantly lower cholesterol levels were seen in the study group boys at age five.

Since atherosclerosis ("hardening" of the arteries) is known to start at a young age, some believe cutting back a bit on saturated fat early in life may make a difference in the long haul. If these kids stay on a lower-saturated-fat diet through the years, will the boys have lower heart disease rates? We may have to wait 50 or 60 years to find out, but the answer will be worth knowing.

For several years I've recommended 2 percent milk for most children starting at age one—unless I have any concerns about a child not eating enough fat. While this may be controversial to some and contradicts the current U.S. guidelines about milk consumption in young children, I believe it's reasonable as long as children are getting adequate amounts of high-quality fats from other sources. Skim milk can be given starting at age two if there are concerns about weight; otherwise, 2 percent is fine.

Don't put children under age two on low-fat diets without consulting your physician or dietitian. This doesn't mean, though, that one-year-olds can't start drinking 2 percent milk as long as they have good quality fat in their diet. Skim milk, however, should be reserved for children age two and over due to its lack of essential fatty acids.

FRIENDLY FATS

When people think of fat, they generally think of animal fat—the kind found in steaks, chicken, pork chops, and bacon. But excellent sources of *healthy* fat abound in foods like olives, avocados, soy products, and various nuts, to name a few.

Cultures adjacent to the Mediterranean Sea, partaking of larger amounts of these plant fats, experience lower rates of heart disease than do countries whose residents consume more animal fat. We should be eating much more "Mediterranean" plant fat and fewer animal fats.

How can you tell "good fats" from "bad fats"? As a general rule, if an oil is liquid at room temperature, it's higher in good, monounsaturated fat. Examples: olive and canola oils. If it's solid at room temperature, it's high in bad, saturated fat. Example: lard.

Have you ever enjoyed a delicious steak for dinner, then set the plates and scraps aside while you sat for a while in the family room? What did you find when you returned an hour later to clean the dishes? Unless the room was really hot, I'd guess you encountered little blobs of less-than-appealing solidified fat where steak juices had been. Saturated fat solidifies as it cools. Bacon grease is another classic example.

I don't mention this to disgust you, but to illustrate a point. And I certainly don't desire the ire of meat producers. I love a good steak now and then, as well as other meats. High quality, trim cuts of meat contain vital nutrients such as iron and provide an excellent source of protein. They're appropriate for children if not given in excess. Portion sizes should be about the size of a deck of cards. Balance and moderation are the key.

When it comes to healthier fat, nuts are an excellent source. Plenty of types are available, so offer a variety. They're appropriate for older children; consult your physician before giving any intact nuts to a younger child, because of the risk of choking.

A complete prohibition on intact nuts may be best until seven years of age. Crushed nuts or nut "butter" can be given earlier. I'd recommend waiting until at least age two before introducing peanut butter, though, due to the severity and prevalence of peanut allergy today.

The jury is still out on the question of whether delaying the introduction of peanut butter may reduce the chance of developing peanut allergy. If you have a family history of food allergies, wait until age three. If you have another child with peanut allergy, it's a moot point; you should not have any peanut products in the house!

WHAT ABOUT ATKINS?

A discussion of fat wouldn't be complete without mentioning the Atkins Diet.

Whether you agree with him or not, the late Dr. Robert Atkins deserves kudos for challenging the medical establishment's assumptions about weight control. In 1972 he published his first book, *Diet Revolution,* advocating a low-carbohydrate diet—and was basically branded a heretic. In 1992, he revised and updated the book, calling it *Dr. Atkins' New Diet Revolution.* His approach was still considered eccentric and possibly dangerous. He wasn't dissuaded, however, as he saw many people losing weight with his plan.

The main criticism of his high-protein, high-fat, low-carbohydrate approach is the potential for future heart disease due to the high fat intake. A lack of fiber and calcium can also be problematic.

Many feel it's difficult to stay on the diet, as the carbohydrate restriction is severe at the beginning and prohibits some healthy foods including certain fruits, vegetables, and grains. As for the risk of heart disease, recent studies seem to indicate that biochemical markers for heart disease (LDL, triglycerides, C-reactive protein) don't worsen and may actually improve with Atkins. This is another jury that's still out, however.

What's the long-term effectiveness, practicality, and safety of the diet? Should you consider it for your youngster?

Dr. Stephen Sondike designed a study using an Atkins-like diet for obese adolescents.[2] Those in the low-carbohydrate arm of the study lost twice as much weight as the control group, and their lipid profiles didn't worsen. Early studies seem to show that people on these diets eat fewer calories

Because there are no definitive studies showing that Dr. Atkins' diet is safe and effective in children, I wouldn't recommend it for yours. Time will tell how it pans out; as I said before, medical research is a slow, often exasperating process.

The plain fact, however, is that if children ate the way they're supposed to, we wouldn't be discussing the Atkins Diet or obesity in general. Why submit our kids to any unproven, possibly unhealthy, and difficult-to-maintain diet method? Why not teach them to eat properly for the rest of their lives?

So let your children eat healthy fat in moderation. They need it for energy, and for some nutrients they can get no other way. Like carbohydrates, some fats are better than others; later we'll work this fact into our no-gimmick program for weight loss and fitness.

PROTEIN PRINCIPLES

Unlike carbohydrates and fat, protein isn't controversial in the weight loss literature. You can find diets advocating less fat and more carbs, or more fat and fewer carbs, but you won't find the low-protein variety. Most people understand the important place protein has in our diets.

High-protein diets were briefly popular in the 1980s. Severe calorie restriction was coupled with increased protein intake to prevent muscle breakdown. The body burned fat for energy. These "protein sparing fasts" were effective for quick weight loss, but not over the long haul. They also had some potentially serious side effects.

Insufficient calorie intake made it nearly impossible for a person to maintain these diets, due to constant hunger. Weight loss researchers have concentrated on fat and carbohydrates in their more recent interventions, keeping protein intake recommendations fairly constant.

Most adults and children consume about 15 percent of their calories in the form of protein. Proteins are the fundamental building blocks of the body. Comprised of various combinations of amino acids, they are meticulously produced by our DNA.

Proteins are constantly being built and broken down in our bodies. The amino acids necessary for making them must be produced in the body or ingested. Like essential fatty acids, certain of these amino acids—essential amino acids—must be obtained in the diet, for they can't be manufactured. If they're lacking, optimal tissue repair can't take place and protein deficiencies will arise.

If your child is eating a reasonably diverse diet, protein deficiency shouldn't be a problem. Eggs, milk, legumes (especially soy), and meat are the best protein sources. I've never seen a case of *primary* protein deficiency (caused by a lack of protein and/or essential amino acids in the diet, in contrast to an internal problem resulting in deficiency) in all my years of practice.

When protein is broken down, nitrogen is one of the by-products. When a person eats enough protein to match what is lost, doctors refer to this as being in "nitrogen balance." Thus, children need to eat enough protein to stay in nitrogen balance and to obtain essential amino acids.

If quality protein sources are offered to children, over time they'll eat what they need in the correct proportions. Again, our bodies have an amazing ability to know what they need and when they need it. I've heard countless times from parents that a picky child will suddenly eat a large amount of a food that he wouldn't touch before. That child may then go back to not eating it for a while. In my mind, the only plausible explanation is that his body somehow recognized a need and acted on it. It shouldn't shock us that God has designed our bodies this way, considering the wonder of their phenomenal complexity.

Foods high in protein tend to have lower glycemic indexes, so they belong in the diet of a heavy child. Three to four servings of dairy per day, coupled with up to seven eggs per week, plus several servings of meat and legumes per week will provide an adequate protein base for your child.

It's unlikely that your children won't eat any of the foods I've just listed. But if they won't, keep the foods available. Your kids will reach for them when their bodies need them.

We're almost done with Nutrition 101. In the next chapter, you'll discover why another food ingredient—fiber—is for kids as well as the rest of us.

CHAPTER SEVEN

THE WONDERS OF FIBER[1]

One of the most potent weapons in our arsenal to combat obesity and promote health is also one of the simplest, least exciting you could imagine—dietary fiber.

Want to guarantee you'll never be invited back to a party? Wish to embarrass your children more than you do already? Just talk publicly about the myriad benefits of fiber.

I don't have to worry about being a social outcast in your circles, though. So I can teach you what you need to know.

FIBER FOUNDATIONS

Fiber is the indigestible part of plant foods, passing through the gut essentially unchanged. It provides no energy (calories) or nutrients, yet its health benefits are legion.

Proper fiber intake results in . . .

- lower rates of heart disease
- lower blood pressure

- lower cholesterol and triglyceride levels
- improved carbohydrate metabolism, causing lower insulin secretion
- lower rates of colon and prostate cancer
- lower rates of diverticulitis
- less constipation
- more of a feeling of satiety after eating, leading to fewer calories eaten
- lower rates of obesity . . .

I could go on. And the only downside is, in some people, an increase in flatulence.

Adequate fiber intake is like regular oil changes in your car. It keeps things running smoothly for as long as possible.

No one disputes the benefits of fiber. But most adults and children in our culture don't get nearly enough of this tremendously healthful substance. For children who are still growing, I recommend [age + seven] grams per day. Thus, a four-year-old should be eating at least eleven grams per day; a ten-year-old should ingest seventeen grams per day or more. This is a minimum; more may be needed if a child suffers from constipation or obesity.

Once a person is fully grown and physically mature, the adult recommendation would hold true: 35 grams or more per day for men, and 25-30 grams daily for women.

Most of us ingest only 25-50 percent of our daily recommended amount of fiber, leaving much room for improvement. With a bit of effort you can determine how much fiber your child consumes each day, but you'll have to start reading labels and adding it up (see Appendix B for help). If your child isn't eating enough fiber, gradually increase the quantity by a few grams per week until you reach your goal.

THE BATHROOM AND BEYOND

There are two types of fiber. *Soluble* fiber dissolves in water; *insoluble* doesn't.

As a general rule, grain and cereal-based foods tend to have insoluble fiber; fruits, vegetables, and legumes have more of the soluble kind. Soluble fiber helps lower cholesterol, reduce blood pressure, lessen the risk of heart disease, and modulate blood sugar. Insoluble fiber mainly affects the gut by decreasing gastrointestinal transit time, aiding digestion, promoting regularity, bulking and softening the stool, facilitating the growth of healthy colon bacteria, and reducing the risk of colon disease.

Most of these benefits are self-explanatory—with the possible exception of gastrointestinal transit time. That's the period between food's entrance into your mouth and its elimination in stool. The longer this takes, the more time waste products spend in your gut—which raises your risk for constipation and long-term problems such as colon cancer. Shorter transit times—as long as diarrhea doesn't result—are definitely healthier.

You can check your children's transit times by feeding them corn one evening and monitoring their stool to see how long it takes to show up. (How's that for a homework assignment?) Their transit time should be 24 hours or less.

I'm not the only one who knows about this ingenious diagnostic tool, of course. I remember a grade-school-age patient who complained of abdominal pain. I suspected she was constipated—a very common scenario. She was fine otherwise, but passed a firm stool with some difficulty once every two or three days (a child receiving adequate dietary fiber might go two to four times a day). After I explained about fiber and bowel habits, the girl's mom asked me how she could determine her child's transit time. Before I could answer, this irregular yet bright child excitedly chimed in, "I'll eat corn and we'll see how long it takes to come out!"

She stole my thunder completely. Ah, the passion of youth.

FIBER AND FRUIT JUICE

I've mentioned this before, but it's worth repeating: It's much better for your child to eat an orange than to drink orange juice, or to eat an apple than to drink apple juice. One of the reasons is fiber.

By eating the apple, your child receives the benefits of the pectin fiber—plus all the phytonutrients that God put in that piece of fruit. By simply drinking the juice, your child absorbs the sugar—resulting in a glucose surge, followed by increased insulin levels. The fiber in the fruit helps to slow the absorption of glucose, leveling out the insulin spike by lowering the glycemic load.

By now you realize these unnecessary insulin surges are best avoided—and may build a foundation for obesity. In fact, fiber may be the key to the success of diets with lower glycemic loads; the fiber in whole grains, legumes, fruits, and vegetables may aid weight loss significantly. Only further research will sort this out.

So keep the grapes, berries, apples, oranges, and grapefruit around the house. Ditch the juices. And speaking of beverages, remind your child to drink plenty of water when increasing fiber intake.

WHAT ABOUT SUPPLEMENTS?

If it proves difficult for your child to eat enough fiber, supplements are available. Many aren't very practical for kids, however, as they come in an unappealing powder or capsule form. Still, there are several workable ways to get extra fiber into your child.

1. Miller's bran—named after the miller of the grain, not Mr. Miller—is simply the fiber left over when grain is processed. Available in bags or boxes at health food stores, it has a flaky consistency and can be sprinkled onto foods or added to recipes.

2. You can buy flax seed (available at health food stores and some supermarkets) and grind it up a bit, adding it to various foods. A coffee bean grinder serves this purpose well. Flax seed contains potent antioxidants, and is loaded with vitamins and essential fatty acids. You'd have trouble finding a better food staple on earth, but you'll be hard-pressed to get your children to eat it straight. It doesn't taste bad, just rather nutty—and takes considerable work and water to get down. By adding lightly ground flax seed to food, however, you can increase your kids' fiber intake and give them an unparalleled source of nutrients.

3. You can buy a high-fiber cereal such as All-Bran or Shredded Wheat and Bran; grind it up and add it to various dishes.

TOO MUCH OF A GOOD THING?

As you increase your child's fiber intake, do it slowly. Otherwise, he or she may complain of gas and cramping and have loose stools.

I made the mistake of inadequately warning my mother about this side effect several years ago when she began fiber supplementation on my advice. She logically figured that since fiber was so healthful and non-toxic, the more the better. She was less than pleased with me after spending the better part of 24 hours sitting in her bathroom, trapped in a painful, bloated funk.

It had been decades since I'd heard her angrily call me "Robert Scott!" But I heard it loud and clear that day, I can tell you.

Sheepish, I joked that you get what you pay for in the advice department, but she wasn't amused. I'm happy to report that she still loves me, though she breaks out in a cold sweat whenever she sees a bran muffin.

Don't go from zero to 60 in 4.9 seconds when it comes to fiber intake. Gradually increasing fiber over a few weeks will help your kids' bodies adjust and avoid bloating. This possible side effect is a small price to pay for the tremendous benefits of fiber in your child's diet.

A BANDWAGON TO JUMP ON

One thing is certain: If our children optimized their fiber intakes by eating more fresh fruits, vegetables, legumes, and unprocessed, whole-grain foods, they'd be far more healthy.

So head to your grocer and look for whole-grain products. Whole grains are simply grains in their natural state, with the fiber-rich bran, endosperm, and germ included. You'll know a food is truly whole-grain when that's the first ingredient listed.

You won't have trouble finding whole grains, as many companies are jumping on the bandwagon. Chains such as Whole Foods have an especially good selection of whole grains, and you can order just about anything online. An Internet search for "whole grain" will yield much information for you to digest, as it were.

That's the story on fiber. You now have enough knowledge of metabolism and nutrition to understand the "whys" behind the no-gimmick guidance you'll find in the rest of this book. It's time for a very important question that only you and your doctor can answer: Is your child obese?

PART FOUR

IS YOUR CHILD OBESE?

CHAPTER EIGHT

SPOTTING OBESITY AND THE METABOLIC SYNDROME

Now let's get to the heart of the matter. Before we can act on a problem, we need to know if a problem exists.

You may be asking yourself, "Is my child really obese?" You may have already answered that question in your mind, but I'd caution you not to jump to conclusions. This is one area in which you definitely want professional guidance. See your physician—and as you do, keep the following observations in mind.

THE DOCTOR'S DIAGNOSIS

Your doctor's first responsibility is to perform a careful history and physical examination to rule out any medical conditions known to cause obesity.

They're quite rare, however. Prader-Willi, Laurence-Moon-Bardet-Biedl, and Cohen Syndromes are among them; children with these conditions have physical characteristics indicating that they don't have simple exogenous obesity.

Hormonal reasons for obesity are uncommon, too—despite many parents' concern that their child has a "thyroid problem" like Grandma Mabel. Hypothyroidism (low thyroid hormone levels) and Cushing's Disease (high cortisol hormone levels) are two of the better-known—but still infrequently occurring—conditions.

Obesity resulting from a problem inside the body—hormonal, chromosomal, or a syndrome—is "endogenous" obesity. That was the case with one of my young patients.

Sam is a friendly, typical boy from a wonderful family. Shy at first, he warms up as you get to know him.

When Sam was seven years old, his mom scheduled him for a regular checkup. She wanted him examined because for several weeks he'd been complaining of feeling tired—and had gained excessive weight. She didn't see anything else worrisome, and said he had no symptoms of diabetes—symptoms with which she was familiar, since her brother had the disease.

Sam told me he was doing well in school, and that he ate and slept normally. But he revealed to me that he moved his bowels every other day or so and that it sometimes was hard to go.

When I examined him, Sam looked a bit tired and his skin was dull. With a height of 46.5 inches and weight of 67 pounds, he had a BMI of 21.8. Two years before, he'd been 44 inches tall and weighed 43 pounds—for a BMI of 15.6.

He'd grown only 2.5 inches in 2.5 years—much less than expected. His height had dropped significantly in percentile, while his weight had increased abnormally. He was now officially obese.

What was causing this poor growth, weight gain, and fatigue? Was it simple exogenous obesity, or was something else lurking?

The key clues: constipation, decrease in growth percentile, obesity, dull skin, tired appearance. With a family history of diabetes, Sam was also at increased risk for other autoimmune disorders such as hypothyroidism. Could that be the culprit?

Sure enough, testing confirmed that Sam did have hypothyroidism. With treatment, he shot up in height and his weight dropped to a normal level.

Sam had signs of a hormonal problem—chiefly, a drop in his growth velocity. The vast majority of overweight children don't have such signs, and a careful history and physical examination generally can distinguish between the two.

HORSE OR ZEBRA?

Most children diagnosed as obese have straightforward, common obesity. As I've noted before, this "exogenous" condition originates from outside the body—from eating too much, as opposed to an internal problem.

Medical school professors are fond of saying, "When you hear hoofbeats, think horses—not zebras." In other words, common conditions are common; rare diseases, rare. While this is good advice, the sharp physician will always be on the lookout for the patient with "stripes."

One favorite professor of mine used to declare, "If you find a barn full of fresh horse manure and don't find a pony right away, keep looking—he's in there somewhere." That was his colorful way of saying that if a child has symptoms strongly suggesting a defined problem but you come up empty diagnostically, don't give up your search.

Hormonal problems in children usually are accompanied by a significant decrease in growth velocity. To know if that's occurred, your physician needs a baseline. A pattern of growth can be established at regular "well child" examinations—one reason pediatricians consider them so vital.

If a child's growth has been steady and the physical exam fails to reveal anything amiss, a diagnosis of common, exogenous obesity is all but assured. Since children with common obesity tend to be taller than their peers, blood work to distinguish endogenous from exogenous obesity is rarely needed. Tests can be used, however, to look for other coexisting problems such as hyperinsulinism, high fasting glucose levels (an early sign of type 2 diabetes), hyperlipidemia, or other signs of the "metabolic syndrome" (more on this at the end of the chapter).

BMI: BETTER THAN A MIRROR

The most common, current, objective criterion for diagnosing obesity stipulates that the child must have a body mass index (BMI) greater than that of 95 percent of children of the same age and sex—the "95th percentile."

BMI is a number that expresses the relationship between a person's weight and height. It's much better to use BMI than simply to look at a child's growth chart. A child can have a seemingly small difference in height and weight percentile, yet a significantly high BMI.

It's not always easy to determine whether a child is overweight by looking at him or her, either. Many parents have a distorted view of how a child's body should look. For instance, it's not unusual to be able to see the outline of most kids' ribs—yet a lot of parents think this is a sign of emaciation.

That's why an objective measurement is so important. Your doctor can *show* you where your child's BMI stands in relation to other children. BMI, the most practical determiner of body fat we have at present, gives us a nice way to express a ratio of weight to height.

For purposes of this book, *obesity* will be defined as greater than or equal to the 95th percentile for body mass index for age and gender. A child with a BMI in the 85th to 94th percentile will be defined as *overweight*. These are terms used by major organizations around the world to categorize childhood weight problems.

Some avoid using the term "obesity" at all, substituting "overweight." They use the term "at risk for overweight" in place of "overweight." Some feel the term "obesity" demeans a child.

While I can understand that position, I respectfully disagree. I'm comfortable with the term "obesity" as I've just defined it; everyone knows what it means, and it confers an appropriate degree of seriousness to the condition. It's by no means a derogatory term, but a medical one.

Some have noted that by defining obesity as at or above the 95th percentile, 5 percent of kids will always be diagnosed as obese no matter how slim children may become in the future. This is theoretically true, if the BMI curves are recalibrated regularly with time. I believe we should leave the curves as they are, though. We can only hope to be successful enough to face that phantom scenario someday, when all children are at an appropriate weight and we're misdiagnosing 5 percent as obese. To paraphrase a popular saying, "That dog is unlikely to hunt."

Some in the U.K. are concerned that weight data are drawn from kids in the United States, and may not accurately reflect every country's norms. But since the U.S. is comprised of such a variety of cultural backgrounds, American statistics probably are as normative as any out there. At the same time, some researchers are making a useful attempt to define obesity with more global input and develop worldwide standards.

CRUNCHING THE NUMBERS

To find out if your child is obese or overweight, calculate his or her BMI. Plot the number on a BMI curve according to age; then see into what percentile the child falls.

BMI curves can be found at the Centers for Disease Control and Prevention's Web site (www.cdc.gov). Find the Clinical Growth Chart link and scroll down to the BMI charts. Look for "Boys BMI-for-age" and "Girls BMI-for-age" for ages 2-20.

You can also use the chart I've put together (see Table 1) with the 75th, 85th, and 95th percentiles for boys and girls.

How do you calculate BMI? Here's the formula, using pounds and inches:

(Weight in pounds) times 703, divided by (height in inches times height in inches)

Here's the formula for those using the metric system:

(Weight in kilograms) divided by (height in meters times height in meters)

If you use the metric calculation, be sure to use *meters*; most doctors who use metric measurements will give you a child's height in *centimeters*. Simply divide centimeters by 100 to obtain meters.

One note of caution when interpreting BMI: A child or adult with a lot of muscle mass may be inaccurately classified as overweight or obese. This occurs because muscle weighs much more per unit volume than fat. Weight lifters, wrestlers, or muscular football players may fall into this category.

I remember a 17-year-old football player I saw for a sports participation exam. Glancing at his chart before I entered the room, I saw that he was 5 feet 11 inches and weighed 186 pounds. His BMI was 26—at about the 90th percentile for his age, which was "technically" overweight. His exam proved that he was nothing of the kind, however. There wasn't an ounce of fat on him; he was solid muscle!

He laughed when I showed him the BMI chart and when I ribbed him that he needed to lose weight. Truth be told, he needed every pound to use against tacklers and blockers. So take muscle mass into account when looking at BMI percentages.

While the 95th percentile for BMI defines obesity, the 85th percentile is the cutoff for defining children as overweight. Obese children are at high risk for becoming obese adults; overweight children are at high risk for becoming obese children and adults.

BMI charts can be a crucial aid in evaluating a child who's overweight or obese. Note that BMI changes with age and differs slightly between girls and boys; the charts take this into account. For example, look at the 75th, 85th, and 95th BMI percentiles for boys and girls at various ages[1] in the following table.

TABLE 1

Age (years)	Boys 75th percentile	Boys 85th percentile	Boys 95th percentile	Girls 75th percentile	Girls 85th percentile	Girls 95th percentile
2	17.6	18.2	19.3	17.4	18.0	19.0
3	16.8	17.4	18.2	16.6	17.2	18.3
4	16.4	17.0	17.8	16.2	16.8	18.0
5	16.3	16.8	17.9	16.1	16.8	18.3
6	16.4	17.0	18.4	16.3	17.1	18.8
7	16.6	17.4	19.1	16.7	17.6	19.6
8	17.0	18.0	20.0	17.3	18.3	20.6
9	17.6	18.6	21.0	18.0	19.1	21.8
10	18.2	19.4	22.1	18.6	20.0	22.9
11	18.9	20.2	23.2	19.4	20.8	24.1
12	19.6	21.0	24.2	20.2	21.7	25.2

TABLE 1 (continued)

Age (years)	Boys 75th percentile	Boys 85th percentile	Boys 95th percentile	Girls 75th percentile	Girls 85th percentile	Girls 95th percentile
13	20.4	21.8	25.2	21.0	22.5	26.3
14	21.2	22.6	26.0	21.7	23.3	27.2
15	22.0	23.4	26.8	22.3	24.0	28.1
16	22.7	24.2	27.5	22.9	24.6	28.9
17	23.4	24.9	28.2	23.4	25.2	29.6
18	24.1	25.6	28.9	23.8	25.7	30.3
19	24.8	26.3	29.7	24.2	26.1	31.0
20	25.4	27.0	30.6	24.4	26.5	31.8

Notice the dip from age two to five as children thin out a bit—and the steady increase thereafter. After 18, boys tend to have a higher BMI—the largest difference being seen at age 20—due to more muscle mass.

Adult BMI percentiles don't apply until age 20. Don't use adult BMI guidelines until that age. Adults use a more general BMI guideline that looks like this:[2]

TABLE 2

BMI	Classification	Medical Risk Assignment
Less than 18.5	Underweight	May be some increased health risk
18.5-24.9	Normal weight for height	Normal risk
25-29.9	Overweight	Medium risk for medical complications
30-34.9	Obese	High risk for medical complications
35-39.9	Very obese	Very high risk for complications
40 or more	Morbidly obese	Extremely high risk

THE METABOLIC SYNDROME

The "metabolic syndrome" is a collection of problems associated with obesity that exist in the same person:

- a high amount of abdominal fat with increased waist size
- glucose intolerance
- insulin resistance
- dyslipidemia (high triglyceride or LDL and/or low HDL levels)
- high inflammation markers (C-reactive protein)
- high blood pressure

You may also see this condition referred to as "syndrome X" or "insulin resistance syndrome."

As the name implies, the affected person's metabolism is out of whack. Diagnostic criteria for the syndrome aren't standardized yet, but most physicians agree that at least three of the aforementioned symptoms need to be present.

The metabolic syndrome is a ticking time bomb of the heart. Those afflicted are at risk for early coronary artery disease and type 2 diabetes.

According to some estimates, up to 25 percent of the adult U.S. population may be affected by the metabolic syndrome. A recent study[3] concluded that almost 30 percent of obese adolescents fulfill the criteria for diagnosis.

The emergence of this syndrome seems mostly due to the poor diets and sedentary ways of many in our society. If you have an adolescent diagnosed with obesity, he or she should have an evaluation to determine if the metabolic syndrome is present. Weight loss and exercise remain the cure for this malady, but problems such as high blood pressure and high cholesterol may need immediate attention.

TAKING ACTION

If you're concerned about your child's weight, calculate BMI. If it's borderline or high, see your doctor for an evaluation.

With a careful history, physical exam, and BMI calculation, your physician should be able to assess your child. If your youngster is diagnosed with obesity, further testing may be in order to see if the metabolic syndrome is present.

If you feel your child is gaining too much weight or doesn't look the right size to you, don't delay. Don't assume that your child will "outgrow" the problem. If he or she is overweight or obese, now's the time to start making some meaningful, lasting lifestyle changes.

We'll consider those changes in Chapters 12-17. But next, we'll look at important principles and practices for all parents—those who want to *prevent* childhood obesity as well as those whose kids are already carrying excess weight.

PART FIVE

STARTING
OUT RIGHT

CHAPTER NINE

THE NEONATAL, INFANT, AND TODDLER YEARS

If you're considering motherhood, you can begin to prevent obesity in your child from before the moment of conception. How? By taking care of yourself.

Mothers-to-be would do well to optimize their health *before* they become pregnant. Studies show that obese women are at higher risk for many problems during pregnancy. Their children run greater risks as well; kids born to overweight moms are more likely to be born too heavy. This is called *macrosomia* (*macro* = big, *soma* = body), and it increases a child's risk of obesity as he or she grows older.[1]

To give a child the best possible start, a mom-to-be should establish healthy eating habits and weight before conception—and continue throughout pregnancy.

THE BENEFITS OF BREAST-FEEDING

Once your child is born, I highly recommend that you breast-feed. Nutritional scientists have been trying for years to make a baby formula

that equals a mother's milk; they keep coming up short as new benefits of breast-feeding are discovered.

Several recent studies have shown that breast-feeding reduces the
risk of obesity in children, and the evidence is growing.[2] Some possible reasons: a baby's intake of breast milk may be better self-regulated
than bottle-feeding; lower protein and increased fat intake may mean
lower insulin levels;[3] breast-feeding may result in lower rates of "leptin resistance" later in life, and may make the body more sensitive to
the benefits of leptin.

"What's leptin?" you may be asking. It's a hormone that helps
regulate appetite. More leptin causes more appetite suppression; with
less leptin, you feel hungry. Some obese individuals may have leptin
resistance, thus not having typical appetite inhibition.

Don't count on leptin to control your child's weight, though.
While studies may shed more light on leptin's role in obesity and even
lead to treatments that help people get started with weight control, for
long-term success you'll still need to follow no-gimmick guidelines on
nutrition and exercise.

I've seen many parents worry that their breast-fed infants aren't
getting enough calories. Some breast-fed infants are chubbier than
their formula-fed peers, but most tend to be a bit leaner. Since infant
growth charts contain data skewed toward formula-fed babies,
breast-fed babies may seem to be growing inadequately by comparison. As they monitor a nursing baby's progress up the growth
chart, these parents ask, "Is it okay that he's below average on the
curve?"

The answer to this question is "Yes." If a baby is nursing well,
seems happy, and is steadily gaining weight, don't worry if he or
she appears lean. Infants are fully capable of self-regulating their
intake.

TWO NEEDLESS WORRIES

We need to squelch the dogma that only a fat baby is a healthy baby. This is simply not true. Yet I can tell you after 18 years in pediatric practice that parents usually view big, chubby infants as healthier than lean ones.

The same is true of doctors, to some degree. It took me a few years before I was really comfortable watching a breast-fed baby slowly fall to the lower percentiles on the growth curve, despite the fact that he or she looked fine.

One family I've known for years comes to mind, and I smile as I write the story. All of the children in the family were breast-fed for the first year or so. All started out near the 25th to 50th percentiles for weight. But over the next few months they dramatically slid down the curve to below the 5th percentile—all while developing normally and acting as happy as can be. They didn't lose actual pounds; they just fell in their weight percentiles.

With the first baby, I ordered a typical battery of tests to make sure nothing was wrong. The results were normal. With the second child, I ordered just a few tests—again with normal results. With the rest of the kids, the mom and I simply laughed about the predictable "dip" in their weight percentiles.

All the kids grew steadily and eventually reached the "normal" part of the chart. None of them is overweight.

It was one of those times when experience enabled everyone to rest assured. This doesn't mean, of course, that you should never be concerned if your breast-fed baby is smaller than her formula-fed peers; every child and family needs its own assessment from a physician.

What about feeding a nursing baby too much? It's nearly impossible to overfeed a breast-fed infant in the first six months. If the baby tries to ingest too much, the mom's milk supply has trouble keeping up. After the milk supply is established, most babies settle into a pattern of nursing every 2-3 hours during the daytime and every 3-4 hours at night.

There is, however, one "back door to obesity" through which parents and a breast-fed child can enter. This happens when a baby develops the habit of nursing every time he wakes up—after the period when he no longer needs to eat at night. This "trained night feeding" usually begins around 6-9 months of age, when the baby has started to eat some solids and is perfectly capable of sleeping through the night.

All babies wake up several times at night, usually going back to sleep without parents even knowing. Sometimes they cry briefly due to separation anxiety or disorientation. If a well-intentioned mom takes this as a sign of hunger and nurses the child, the baby may come to expect a feeding whenever he awakens. If this continues, the infant consumes extra calories—which add up.

A "tough love" approach—in which the baby is taught to go back to sleep on his own without nursing—remains the best, quickest remedy. With a full night's sleep, both baby and mom are happier.

IS TIMING EVERYTHING?

How long should you plan on nursing? Will you further lower the risk of obesity for your baby the longer you breast-feed?

The short answer is that we don't know.

Based on current data, I'd recommend exclusive nursing for at least four to six months. Whether or not nursing for longer periods will offer increased protection against obesity, the other benefits of breast-feeding are so numerous that you'd be wise to nurse for at least a year.

It's not known whether any long-term benefits continue to accrue after that, and it's very hard to design studies that answer this question with certainty. If babies breast-fed for 18 months were to show lower rates of obesity than those nursed until a year, would it be due to the milk or to family factors? Would nursing 100 percent versus 75 percent make a difference? Variables like these make it unlikely that we'll reach definitive conclusions anytime soon.

If at the one-year point you and your baby are enjoying the interaction and he or she is thriving, continue to nurse. There's no set time to wean. Most of the time it will be apparent when you and your child are ready.

IS NURSING FOR YOU?

If you didn't breast-feed your baby, this isn't a time for guilt or self-condemnation. But understanding the research may encourage you to nurse your next child—or to be a gracious advocate for breast-feeding in your circle of influence.

If you were born into a family challenged by weight problems and you need a reason to breast-feed your infant, you have it. If you did breast-feed, don't assume you've done all you can to prevent obesity. Nursing is just one factor affecting a child's weight.

I believe breast-feeding should be encouraged for all moms, and supported strongly in those who want to nurse their babies. Breast milk will always be the ideal food for infants; nothing humans make will ever match what God designed.

FORMULA FEEDING

Moms who can't breast-feed, or who choose not to, should use a quality infant formula. Select one that has the important fatty acids

ARA and DHA added; these nutrients enhance brain and eye development. Found in breast milk, they've only recently been added to formula.

The formula you choose should also be "with iron." Iron fortification brings the formula's iron content up to the correct level; it doesn't mean excessive amounts have been added. Despite stories you may have heard, there's no evidence that iron-fortified formula causes excess gas, constipation, or colic. Since iron plays a vital role in an infant's development, it makes no sense to risk deficiency by using a "low-iron" formula.

One of the most common—and understandable—mistakes I see parents make is overfeeding a formula-fed baby. Mistaken advice from relatives and misinterpreted cries from infants are but two causes.

Babies cry for a myriad of reasons. But in the middle of the night, with a seemingly inconsolable infant, many parents assume the baby is hungry—and feed him despite the fact that he's eaten recently. When he gulps down another four ounces and seems a bit better, the parents figure they were right.

Maybe—but not necessarily. A baby in distress from colic or other causes will often drink anything given to him; being pacified, rather than having hunger satisfied, may have calmed him down. Overfeeding also can cause abdominal pain; if a too-full infant's crying is interpreted as hunger, feeding him again will only perpetuate the problem.

How do you avoid these snares? For years I've taught parents to place reasonable limits on how much formula they feed their babies. I've found that often we have to adjust downward for smaller babies, but rarely do we have to boost intake for bigger ones.

The guidelines I suggest to parents are as follows:

TABLE 3

Age	Maximum amount per feeding, assuming a feeding every 3-4 hours
Birth to 2 weeks of age	3 ounces
2 weeks to 2 months	4 ounces
2 months to 3 months	5 ounces
3 months to 4 months	6 ounces
4 months to 5 months	7 ounces
5 months to 6 months	8 ounces
6 months and above	8 ounces per feeding; 32 ounces per day

From 6 months to a year, never give more than 8 ounces per feeding or more than 32 ounces per day. This is more than enough formula for a normal infant. Will she sometimes seem a bit hungry or fussy? Yes. Should your first response be to increase the size or frequency of her feedings? No!

When it comes to eating habits, infants resemble my late golden retriever, Cody. Like Cody, babies are absolutely thrilled with such a simple thing as a meal. It was touching to be so appreciated for putting kibble in his bowl. We had to watch how much we fed Cody, or he'd eat too much and gain excess weight. To a degree, the same holds true for infants.

Sometimes babies will make it known when they've had enough, but not always. So be a bit careful in feeding them. As long as your child is growing and developing normally, you need not worry about "starving" him or her.

If you choose formula, continue it until your child is a year old. Cow's milk is not appropriate for children under age one.

JUNK THE JUICE

Bulletin: Juices do not constitute a necessary component of an infant or child's diet.

This may shock some parents, but it's a fact. Some believe fruit juice is "healthier" than other sweet drinks such as soda pop. But the "natural" sugar in juice has the same effect on insulin secretion as soda pop does.

What about the vitamins in juice? The vitamin C and the few other nutrients found in juice can easily be obtained from other sources. Some juices—apple and prune—may be helpful temporarily for a constipated child, but that's the extent of their usefulness.

How about the cute little spill-proof juice boxes kids can carry around? I admit they're quite convenient. But so are bottles of water. Go with the water.

Since juices don't give a child a feeling of fullness, a child will eat just as much as she would have without the juice. Thus, juice simply "mainlines" sugar into a child's body. Youngsters quickly become "hooked" on the sweet taste of juice and may never be happy again with plain water.

Many toddlers and older children suffer obesity partly because they became "juice-aholics" as infants. It's so unnecessary; it would be hard to find a child in our society suffering health problems for his lack of fruit juice.

I strongly recommend not letting your children board the juice train. A little fresh orange or grapefruit juice with breakfast when they get older won't upset the balance of the universe. But the less accustomed they become to sweet, sugary drinks—and the more they get used to drinking water—the better for them.

One little girl I cared for was a dramatic picture of what can happen when children consume sugar-laden drinks—juice or otherwise. Rafaela was a beautiful child whose parents were recent immigrants from Mexico. I saw her for a respiratory illness when she was two years old.

Before I entered the room, I could see from her chart that she had a problem much greater than her current virus. Rafaela was quite overweight. She weighed 41 pounds; her BMI of 21 was very high for a two-year-old. Curious, she looked up through soulful, big brown eyes as I introduced myself to her mom.

After a few minutes of getting acquainted and taking Rafaela's history, I began to examine her. That's when her "doctor anxiety" kicked in. She went ballistic, as many two-year-olds do when confronted with such scary creatures as pediatricians.

Before I could get the stethoscope into my ears to protect my cochlea from the auditory assault, mom had reached into her bag. Producing a huge cup of a white liquid, she gave it to Rafaela. It was a clear attempt to quiet the girl down, and it worked.

I assumed the drink was milk. But I asked the mom anyway, curious to know the magical liquid's composition.

"*Horchata*," came her reply.

Horchata? I knew what *leche* meant in Spanish. Was *horchata* a Spanish synonym for *leche*, i.e., milk?

As mom explained to me what *horchata* was, the origin of Rafaela's obesity became clear. *Horchata* is a milk-like drink made from white rice and sugar—and loaded with calories!

Mom had been giving *horchata* to Rafaela as a liquid pacifier since the girl's infancy. Parents who use juice for the same purpose will get a similar result.

Rafaela did better over the next few years as her consumption of sugar decreased, but I lost her to follow-up. She'll probably battle this problem for a lifetime, all because of a lack of information on the part of her well-meaning, first-time mom.

For your children's sake, please don't make the same mistake.

INTRODUCING SOLIDS

With proper vitamin supplementation, infants can thrive perfectly on breast milk alone for the first six months. Adding vitamin D to the child's diet is now recommended to help breast-fed infants improve calcium absorption.

Families with a history of allergic disease, eczema, asthma, or obesity should consider exclusive nursing for the first five to six months. This should allow the child's digestive tract to mature, reducing the risk of intact proteins being absorbed into the bloodstream—which can lead to food allergies.

Exclusive nursing for *longer* than five to six months has been shown to be ineffective in reducing the conditions I've just listed. If you're using formula, your baby could thrive on formula alone, without vitamins, for the first six months.

In otherwise healthy, non-allergic families, there's nothing wrong with introducing a little rice cereal to your baby at four months of age. Start slowly and modestly, mixing a few tablespoons of cereal with formula or breast milk to give it a thick-soup texture. Gradually increase the texture and amount. In a few weeks, add a second daily feeding. I recommend serving cereal at breakfast or dinner, not at bedtime.

Speaking of cereal, what about whole grains for babies? Great question!

Despite all we've learned about the benefits of whole grains and low-glycemic-load foods, the baby food industry is still a little behind the times. People hesitate to change things when it comes to babies. Parents and doctors—myself included—get comfortable with routines.

Since the bran of a grain isn't digested or absorbed, I see no increased allergy risk to a baby from eating whole grains; that risk comes from protein, not bran. If a child is going to be allergic to a grain, he or she will be allergic to the processed grain as well as the whole form. Whole grains certainly would lower glycemic loads and help prevent constipation in babies and toddlers; we pediatricians battle constipation in our young ones all the time.

Unfortunately, no whole-grain baby cereals are commercially available at this writing. I know several moms who've prepared them at home, though, using brown, whole-grain rice, and whole, rolled oats. If you have the time and inclination, I think this is a great idea. Cook the grains; then grind them to the consistency you desire for your baby.

Before four months of age, most infants aren't neurologically or immunologically ready for solid food feeding. Some parents might protest, "But if I don't give him cereal at bedtime, he won't sleep through the night!" Trust me: He'll start sleeping through the night when he's good and ready, cereal or not.

As I've already mentioned, I don't recommend giving cereal before bedtime anyway. Avoid letting a child develop a habit of eating solids right before falling asleep. "Habit" snacks before bed can increase the likelihood of obesity.

It's perfectly okay, though, for an infant to nurse or have some formula before going to sleep. It's best to finish the feeding before the baby falls asleep; burp him, and while he's still awake yet drowsy, lay him down to sleep.

What about the "stages" for solid foods, the ones marked on jars of baby food? I recommend stage 2 foods at about 6-7 months of age, and stage 3 around 8-9 months.

Stage 1 foods are single-ingredient foods pureed to be very smoothly textured, appropriate for a child learning to swallow solids. Stage 2 foods have a bit more texture, come in slightly larger portions, and contain combinations of foods. Stage 3 offerings are more like table foods, designed for babies who are experienced eaters.

When you introduce stage 1 foods—about one or two months after starting cereal—begin with vegetables. Work your way through those before starting fruits. Buy a brand with no added sugar. I like my patients to learn to enjoy vegetables before having their palates tantalized with sweeter things like fruit.

My experience has been that by the time babies are ready for stage 3, they want the real McCoy, right from the table. That's fine. "No more of this bland baby food stuff for me, Bub," you can see them thinking. Seldom do parents tell me that their babies are happy with stage 3 foods.

THE NEED FOR LESS SPEED

Feed as slowly as you can, making it an enjoyable, interactive experience.

As soon as you see your baby losing interest or beginning to spit out spoonfuls, stop. Remember that there's a delay of about 20 minutes from the time your stomach is full to the time your brain realizes it. This delay in sensing when you're full is a key concept to grasp.

Let me illustrate. Have you ever felt really hungry and had a fresh, hot pizza placed in front of you? Maybe you proceeded to devour half of it in about 10 minutes.

You continued to feel hungry, though. Since the pizza still looked and smelled delicious, you ate a few more pieces. After all, you didn't want it to get cold.

But 20 minutes later, you never wanted to look at another pizza again.

How could something so tasty make you feel so stuffed and terribly uncomfortable? Now you know why. You ate so fast that your brain didn't have time to sense when you were full—until it was too late.

This explains why eating slowly is helpful: You feel full *before* overeating. Mom's sage advice about chewing each bite umpteen times was prescient—but not for the reason she thought. It wasn't just that complete mastication was beneficial; it was the fact that it slowed you down.

This is very important, since overweight children have to eat less. Teach them to eat slowly, and their intake will decrease.

MAKING YOUR OWN BABY FOOD

Nothing says that you can't make your own baby food.

If you're unfamiliar with the stages, buy a few jars to see what the textures are like. Then prepare the food, grind it to the desired smoothness, and place it in ice cube trays. Cover and freeze. When needed, you can remove one, two, or three cubes, heat slowly in a saucepan, and serve.

Most children can also begin eating some soft table food by 8-9 months of age. If they seem interested and have good hand-to-mouth developmental skills, they can begin to feed themselves some of the time.

The most important thing to keep in mind: Don't give a baby anything that could choke her by lodging in the windpipe should she suck it in. All babies will *gag* at times when eating, but if you avoid small, hard foods, you'll prevent serious choking.

We're probably a bit overcautious when it comes to how slowly we introduce foods. Parents in some other cultures feed their kids earlier and with much spicier foods, and it doesn't seem to result in any more problems.

Every family has its own comfort level where baby food is concerned. Keep things soft and proceed deliberately. Use common sense; consult with your doctor if you're unsure what is appropriate fare.

As your infant grows, think carefully about what you feed her. Allow her to experience the "fun" stuff, but in moderation. What would your baby's first year be without a birthday party picture of her smiling with cake frosting smeared all over her face?

Offer your youngster a good variety of foods with different colors, textures, and flavors. Remember that it takes dozens of tastings before a child truly becomes comfortable with a food. That's why you should keep offering wholesome foods, even if the child rejects them over and over.

So here are five tips to remember:
- avoid sugar-laden foods, including juices
- eat together as a family
- feed your little one slowly
- avoid solid foods before bed
- don't let your child have a bottle in the crib; the crib is for sleeping, period

TODDLER CHALLENGES

The toddler years usually bring some surprises and curve balls. Children who were fantastic eaters often develop a propensity toward pickiness.

Don't let this throw you for a loop. Given access to a good variety of foods, kids *will* eat enough to grow. We humans possess a very accurate hunger mechanism that causes us to eat when we're hungry.

The key is to let a child eat based on internal hunger clues, not external cajoling. Never entreat a child to "clean your plate" or offer dessert as a reward for finishing dinner. By doing so, you substitute an external reward—dessert or parental approval—for the child's internal satiety mechanism.

Did you ever hear from your parents, "Eat all your food; there are children starving in China"? I realize that my parents only wanted me to be thankful for having enough food, and I'm sensitive to the reality of hunger around the world. But this isn't the appropriate way to motivate your kids to eat. Eating more than they need will only make your children overweight; it won't help a child in another country who may not have enough. Self-regulating intake is vital, especially in toddlers, and encouraging them to keep eating when they're no longer hungry discourages self-regulation.

Don't fall into the trap of allowing a determined two-year-old to rule the house and the dinner table, making everyone else miserable. Toddlers, who are egocentric, behave in a way that they believe will get them what they want. If they learn that one behavior won't produce the desired result, they'll try a different approach.

Similarly, if their behavior causes an undesired consequence—a time-out, loss of privilege, or parental disapproval—they'll eventually abandon it. Keep that in mind when dealing with a whiny or recalcitrant toddler.

Transition your toddler from bottle to cup as soon as possible. Don't let him "own" the cup and carry it around all day like a favorite toy, though; you need to be in charge of its use.

As for your toddler's menu, starting at one year a child can begin to drink 2 percent milk and eat more and different table foods. Aside from choking risk and allergic hazard, the sky's the limit.

FOOD FIGHTS AND FINICKY EATERS

Here are two truths about toddlers and food:

1. You can't force children to eat.
2. They eventually realize this fact.

If mealtimes are tense, your child may be using them in a power ploy to aggravate you. What should you do?

If, after a leisurely meal, your child hasn't finished or plays with his food, take it away. Find a balance between eating too quickly and dawdling. Your child soon will learn not to play with his food.

If your toddler throws food, don't give it back to her or replace it. Warn her about food throwing. If she repeats her performance, calmly end the meal and let her go hungry until the next one. This is not a "mean" thing to do, but common-sense discipline. Consequences are, by far, the best teacher.

It's typical for toddlers and preschoolers to eat a good breakfast and lunch, only to refuse dinner. This may be because breakfast and lunch foods are naturally more appealing to many young children. Whatever the reason, offer a good variety of foods at all meals if you can. If your child has a poor appetite for dinner, don't let him snack during the three hours before the meal—and offer nothing to eat afterward.

Toddlerhood is the time when you want to start shaping children's thinking about food. For instance, give them whole-grain bread so they come to see it—and not the white variety—as "normal."

When I was growing up, the only time I saw whole-grain bread was at Grandpa and Grandma Andersen's house. I assumed it wasn't available in my town, and could be found only at Grandma's supermarket. After refusing to eat it for a while, I began to look forward to "brown bread" at her house—even though I mistakenly thought only white bread was "real" bread.

Whatever your children learn to eat at a young age will become "normal" to them. Give them high-fiber cereals and non-instant oatmeal early on, so that they don't develop a taste for high-sugar cereals. Mix in some bananas, blueberries, or raspberries. Serve as many fresh fruits and vegetables as your kids will eat; avoid the canned fruits packed in corn syrup or high-fructose syrup.

If you're blessed with a very finicky child, it's okay to give him a multivitamin as a hedge and for your peace of mind. Don't call the vitamins "candy," however. Vitamins can be dangerous and even fatal if a child gets hold of a bottle and eats a handful.

Don't give up if your child rejects a new food. As previously noted, it can take up to a dozen or more tastes before a child accepts a new flavor. Don't feed the child his favorite foods constantly, or he'll never try anything new.

If your youngster won't eat at a meal or two, he'll be fine—just hungrier at the next. If children complain of hunger, there's nothing wrong or cruel about making them wait for an hour or two until the next meal. Calm reassurance and not heeding their whining will help teach them to be patient; a little hunger won't hurt them.

IT ALL ADDS UP

Lastly, avoid using what I call "cracker pacifiers"—constantly giving children animal crackers, saltine crackers, Goldfish, etc., just to keep them quiet or occupied.

Worse are cracker pacifiers with "juice chasers." Throw away the juice boxes!

Just because some of these snack foods don't have much added sugar, are not "candy," or are "low-fat," it doesn't mean they're healthy or can't cause significant glycemic loads and insulin secretion. A little each day can add up to a significant number of unnecessary calories over a year—which can help make the difference between fitness and obesity.

CHAPTER TEN

THE PRESCHOOL, ELEMENTARY, AND PRETEEN YEARS

T rain up a child in the way he should go, and when he is old he will not depart from it" (Proverbs 22:6).

This is a principle, not a promise. But this wisdom from God is as true today as when it was penned. Children need training by their parents in all matters of life, and diet is no exception.

People usually learn how and what to eat in the first 12 years, and habits formed early prove difficult to break. As a parent, you have a unique opportunity to teach your children correct eating routines, and you must do this when they're young.

Some parents seem to forget a basic truth: Generally speaking, your kids can eat only what you have in the house. So if there are foods you don't want them to eat, simply don't buy them. If food is in the house, it will be eaten!

Many times I've been working or studying late, and out of sheer restlessness have gotten up and foraged for food. I really wasn't hungry—just tired or bored. Because my wife is savvy and interested in

my health, she keeps the cabinets largely free of junk food. So my for-
aging usually goes unrewarded.

Admit it: The same thing happens to you, and your children are
no different. They'll eat out of boredom or restlessness. Make it hard
for them; keep them from munching on junk food by not buying it.

By not purchasing unwholesome foods, you'll also model proper
eating habits. Make these your mottoes: "Quality, not quantity"; "Eat
to live, don't live to eat."

And don't lose sleep about your kids eating enough. They will.

THE PRESCHOOL YEARS

In this phase, your kids grow verbal enough to converse with you
about food. They'll be a captive audience until they spend more time
at friends' houses—and you'll lose some control over their intake. Stay
focused in these early years. Teach your kids with a loving spirit and
lead by example.

As I've noted before, body mass index (BMI) tends to fall from
age two to five years. This means your child should lose some of that
cute "baby fat" and begin to look thinner. Parents who don't know
about this natural growth pattern, especially those who have picky
eaters, often become unnecessarily concerned.

Like toddlers, preschoolers tend to be finicky and don't eat much.
They're also accomplished at letting you know when a food tastes
"yucky." Parents must be careful not to take this personally—especially after spending an hour preparing a meal.

My wife and I learned this lesson over 20 years ago as new parents. Our oldest daughter, Heather, was a preschooler. Cheryl prepared a lovely meal one evening; after unsuccessfully cajoling Heather
to try a bite or two of the main dish and watching some fascinating

facial contortions, Cheryl became a bit exasperated. How could the girl refuse this culinary masterpiece? It wasn't exotic, just a good old American dinner.

We proceeded to be more forceful. Heather, being the compliant child that she was, reluctantly took a big bite and swallowed it.

Our insistence turned out to be a bad move. Heather retched mightily, depositing the bite of food—and considerably more—onto the table. Our appetites disappeared for the evening.

And we never forced her to eat anything again.

You don't have to repeat our mistake. Prepare quality meals and serve them to your children; they'll decide whether to eat what you make. You serve, they decide. If they don't eat, let them go hungry. It's only temporary; they'll quickly learn to eat what you make.

That's not easy to do if you've adopted a "Better that he eat something than nothing" mind-set. Some parents succumb to a child's requests for his favorite foods, worried that if they decline, the child will starve himself. They imagine seeing themselves on the 10 o'clock news ("Emaciated children found in the home of Mr. and Mrs. . . ."). Not wanting to become subjects of an abuse inquiry, they give in.

Don't get sucked into this trap. Once you begin making peanut butter sandwiches or macaroni and cheese every night, it's hard to turn back. Remember, you're not short-order cooks. The Proverbs verse doesn't say, "Children, train up your parents in the way they should go."

Assuming a normal neurological and emotional state, your child won't starve himself. God has designed our bodies with a wonderful feedback mechanism that tells us when we need to eat and when we're full.

Offer your child a healthy, well-balanced diet. Allow appetite to determine the quantity, which will likely be less than you desire. I believe that if parents would adhere to these recommendations, most children would eat less junk food and more quality foods. And we'd see fewer overweight youngsters.

THE ELEMENTARY AND PRETEEN YEARS

Consider packing lunches for your kids; avoid having them eat school lunches. School menus are notoriously high in unhealthy fats and high-glycemic-index carbohydrates. They tend to mimic fast food, with an occasional vegetable offering. You can prepare your children much more wholesome meals and exert more control over what they eat.

When I attended grade school and junior high, I walked home at lunchtime each day. The meal typically consisted of a bologna or peanut butter and jelly sandwich with an apple, milk, and occasionally a cookie or two. Special occasions saw a Dolly Madison cherry pie come my way (I don't recommend them, but at age seven I thought they were the pinnacle of fine dining). If Mom was working, she packed me a lunch. Batman and Superman lunch boxes were all the rage, but most of the time I brought a brown paper sack.

I never felt neglected over not receiving a school-prepared lunch. I figured everyone in the world ate a sandwich at lunchtime. To this day I eat a sack lunch on most days, though the sack goes inside a small cooler with a reusable icepack.

Too many of our kids have come to expect a large "hot lunch," usually high in fat and processed carbohydrates, and with many more calories than they need. I think we really do a disservice to kids by expecting schools to replace parents in this area of lunches.

Consider a young lady named Annie, whom I've seen since she was born. At age six, Annie is gregarious, loquacious, and assertive. She had no health problems until age four, when I noticed a slight increase in her weight percentile.

Her mom and I discussed diet and exercise. But at age 6 Annie was 50 inches tall and weighed 85 pounds; her BMI of 23.9 ranked her as officially obese.

Annie was growing taller and had no signs of a physical abnormality that might account for the weight gain. But she'd been eating hot lunches at school and having snacks daily when she came home. In addition, her parents were divorced; she and her frequently traveling dad usually went out for fast food when he was around.

At my request, mom researched the menu at school. The usual culprits dominated the list: hot dogs, pizza, hamburgers, macaroni and cheese. When mom saw where Annie was on the BMI chart, she was convinced of the need for change.

As a full-time teacher and single parent, Annie's mom found it tough to keep track of Annie's diet. Still, mother and daughter got to work and began to walk regularly and watch what they ate. Mom packed Annie a lunch each day. Sugary drinks and most snacks and junk food were deleted from the girl's diet.

Annie's weight gain stopped. Six months later, she'd grown 1.25 inches while her weight had stayed the same—85 pounds. Her BMI had fallen to 22.7. Her weight is still much too high, but has stabilized.

It won't be easy for Annie and her mom. Overweight children in homes affected by divorce have emotional issues to deal with, as well as attempting to lower their BMI. Eating can become a source of comfort in such cases. To turn things around, Annie's older sister, dad, and extended family will need to help. All who care for Annie will need to make changes to ensure her success, making healthy routines not just something they "do" but something they live.

So now that you're going to pack those lunches, what kinds of foods should you include?

I'll give you more detail in chapter 16, but a good, basic lunch would include a sandwich on whole-grain bread, a piece of fruit, and milk. For children older than seven and who aren't allergic, a variety of nuts make an excellent lunch component, too. Packed with vitamins, high in energy, and with a low glycemic index, nuts have in the past been taboo for those wishing to lose weight. But even though they're high in calories relative to their size, they help stave off hunger and insulin surges.

Offer a variety—sunflower seeds, almonds, peanuts, pecans, and walnuts, to name a few. Keep portion sizes small. Generally, a palm-sized helping (about two tablespoons) is the most someone should eat at once.

To see the benefit of adding nuts to your child's diet, try the following for about a week. Add seven or eight whole almonds to your regular breakfast. See if you don't feel satisfied longer. I routinely add almonds to my cereal each morning, and find this to be true. To save money, buy larger quantities of nuts at discount or health food stores. Store them in airtight plastic containers and they'll keep for a long time.

One ingredient to leave *out* of those lunches—and to avoid in general—is sweetened beverages. This includes not only pop, but "sports drinks" like Gatorade and PowerAde. These may be appropriate for heavily sweating athletes, but not for kids who are simply thirsty.

Many parents who wouldn't dream of giving their children pop don't hesitate to let them down sucrose-laden sports drinks at will. I'm sure these parents and their kids believe it's good to drink the stuff they see advertised by professional athletes. But pop is sold by movie stars and sports icons, too.

Common sense and recent data[1] have shown a direct correlation between sweetened beverage intake and weight gain. The same study demonstrated that as sweetened drink (including "pure" fruit juice) consumption increased, milk intake decreased. That meant lower intake of protein, calcium, phosphorus, magnesium, zinc, and vitamins A and D. As you'll see later in this book, calcium is an especially important mineral for children.

Since pop is likely to be the most overconsumed sweet drink for your grade school student or preteen, don't keep it around. Any sweetened beverage intake should be reserved strictly for a treat or special occasion.

What about diet soda pop? I'm inclined to think it's usually best avoided. I disagree, however, with those who believe that aspartame (the sweetener in most diet drinks) will cause the end of civilization as we know it. Use common sense and moderation. In the end, water is by far the best thing for kids to drink when they're thirsty.

WHEN TRAINING PAYS OFF

As children get older, they spend more time visiting friends. You begin to lose a bit of control over what they eat. If you've taught them well, though, you have reason to hope they'll make good choices.

Will they make mistakes and frustrate you at times? Count on it.

For now, control what you keep in your house. It will be a few more years before your child can drive to the store or the burger joint. To minimize the chance that visits with friends will sabotage your efforts, talk with the parents of your child's friends. You can request confidentiality, but let them know if you're engaged in a weight loss effort and that any help they can offer is welcome. You may want to ask them not to let kids eat junk food at their house when your child is there.

The teenage years present some special challenges. That's why that time of life gets special treatment—in the next chapter.

CHAPTER ELEVEN

THE TEENAGE YEARS

It's one thing to tell your five-year-old that you're banning Twinkies from your pantry. It's quite another to try wrestling those golden bundles of fat and sugar from a sixteen-year-old who just drove himself home from the convenience store.

Treating a teenager like a preschooler doesn't work. So how can you get your adolescent to listen when you propose healthier habits?

Let's start to answer that question by looking at some common-sense truths about teens.

ADOLESCENCE: A NEW FRONTIER

Young children need to be dealt with concretely; you can't reason with two-year-olds. Since they can't understand abstractions, you must use the "If . . . then" principle: If this happens, then that consequence will occur.

As kids grow, though, they're increasingly able to understand the reasons behind the rules. This process continues into the late teen years. Even older teenagers may not be able to fully comprehend some of your explanations for the boundaries you set. But more and more, they need to be treated as adults—trusted to make proper decisions on their own in areas like how to spend their free time. You start with choices that have fewer natural consequences and progress to those that have more.

Driving is an example of an activity with potential for extreme danger. But it's something kids need to learn. They'll make plenty of wrong choices; we all have, and the acorns don't fall far from the tree!

Unhealthy habits of eating and exercise can have serious consequences, too. But that doesn't mean you'll be able to keep your teen from making mistakes, minor and major.

Through it all, you need to tell your teen regularly—and demonstrate consistently—that you love her unconditionally, despite what she may have done. Your motivation for discipline must always be your love for her, and she needs to see it in your speech and actions.

Ultimately, you want your child—regardless of age—to be motivated by a love for God and for you, and not primarily by fear of punishment. This is how God wants us to be motivated, too. He's not impressed if we refrain from stealing, lying, and injuring others simply to avoid fines or jail time. He wants us to avoid wrong and do right because we're grateful to Him for sending His Son to rescue us, and because we love others. Imagine what the world would be like if just one biblical injunction were heeded: "You shall love your neighbor as yourself" (Romans 13:9).

If your teen has a relationship with God, she probably can understand and act on those motivations more readily than a young child can. Whether she does depends partly on how you approach the subject of lifestyle changes.

Too many parents attempt to drive their kids' actions legalistically,

using fear of punishment and hope of reward, neglecting issues of attitude and relationship. If you only impose law on your teen, you invite
rebellion.

If you doubt me, put a sign in your yard that says, "Do not throw
stones at front window." Be prepared, however, to call the window
man.

God has placed us "under grace" and not "under law" (Romans
6:14; Galatians 3:10-24). Likewise, as our children enter adolescence,
we increasingly need to appeal to them in terms of grace and gratitude. That's true whether we're trying to guide their choices in dating,
friendships, clothing, music, education—or fitness.

FITNESS AND REBELLION

Attempting to drastically whip your teen's diet into shape is a high-
risk strategy I'd caution against. Getting too strict at this age is likely
to ignite resistance.

This doesn't mean you can't lead by example, however. And it
doesn't mean you can't keep your home free of the unhealthy, fat-
producing fare so many have grown to love.

Focus on reinforcing the benefits of eating healthful food, rather
than nagging your teen about bad food. Parental proscriptions often
make a banned item all the more desirable; the simple act of saying
"No" often leads a youngster to look harder for ways around the
barrier.

So it's better, for example, to keep soft drinks out of your home
than to have them in the refrigerator and forbid their consumption.
Keep candy and cookie supplies low or nonexistent. For snacks, have
some fresh fruit and nuts around rather than potato chips, pretzels,
and fried mozzarella sticks.

HEALTH AND HECTIC SCHEDULES

Between homework loads, extracurricular activities, video games, and late-night instant messaging, a lot of teenagers lead lives that work against becoming and staying fit.

I've seen many students complain of fatigue, headaches, and feeling sick at school. Lack of sleep was a major reason; a significant number also were eating poorly. Simple improvements in their diets made a world of difference; the waves of drowsiness, frequent headaches, and feelings of nausea often disappeared when kids began to eat more fiber, less sugar, and fewer high-GI foods.

Make sure your student gets up early enough to eat a good breakfast every day. I realize this is a difficult proposition; some teens are less than human upon awakening, and may need to hit the snooze button a few times before climbing out of bed. I have experience in this arena with one of my own brood, who shall remain nameless.

Nonetheless, it's been shown repeatedly that a substantial breakfast cuts down on snacking and food cravings throughout the day—and improves school performance. Fresh-cooked oatmeal (you can add a few raisins, berries, or sucralose for sweetness, plus nuts if desired), high-fiber cereals, whole-grain toast, fresh fruits, and eggs all make good choices.

Students who consume a nourishing breakfast each day are more likely to be happier, healthier, and at less risk for becoming overweight. Reaching this goal can be harder if your teen has developed the bad habit of eating right before bedtime, which may decrease his hunger upon awakening. Discourage your child from eating after dinner, and the chances are greater that he'll be hungry by breakfast.

If possible, prepare a lunch each day for your teen. A sandwich of lean turkey or beef with a slice of cheese on whole-grain bread, whole-grain crackers, a few assorted nuts, and an apple or other fresh fruit would be a good example of a healthy, low-glycemic-load lunch. As with younger children, avoid standard school cafeteria fare.

Eat together as a family whenever you can. Frantic schedules make this a challenge, but it promotes good eating habits as well as family cohesion. You may have to move dinnertime later to accommodate everyone, but it's worth it if you can offer your children a more wholesome and more relaxed meal.

TEEN TENACITY: BETH'S STORY

Given the independent nature of most teens, tackling weight problems works best when the motivation comes from within. The determination (or stubbornness, depending on your point of view) many adolescents show can work to their advantage in this area.

One 14-year-old patient, Beth, and her dad saw us a few years ago for a sports participation physical. She was feeling fine, had no complaints, and was happy with school and how things were going. She was trying out for her high school dance squad.

It was apparent that Beth was heavy. This didn't seem to concern her or her dad, though. Both her parents were tall and fairly lean.

The exam showed that Beth was healthy, except for her weight. At 65.75 inches tall and 180 pounds, she had a BMI of 29.3—greater than the 95th percentile.

After I explained this to Beth and her dad, they seemed to grasp that she was obese. As with most overweight kids, the change had been so gradual that the parents hadn't noticed. (Often kids wear clothing that hides extra pounds; parents who *do* notice tend to hope the weight gain will stop and don't act until the youngster is obese.)

We counseled Beth about increasing her Total Daily Energy Expenditure and decreasing her caloric intake. Resolute about exercise, she began to run and weight train. She cut out most junk food and followed our recommendations to increase fiber intake, eliminate high-glycemic-index foods, and substitute healthier fat for the saturated kind. She continued to indulge in typical teenage fare on weekends, however.

The results were dramatic. Six months later she'd grown a half inch and lost 13 pounds. At age 15 she'd grown to 67.5 inches and dropped to 149 pounds. Her BMI was 23—about the 75th percentile.

Beth has continued to work out and eat fairly well, though she admits to eating more "teenager" foods recently. At age 16 she was still 67.5 inches tall and 131 pounds—BMI 20.2. Looking and feeling great, she smiled and talked during the entire exam. She believes her weight is now ideal, and doesn't feel she's still too heavy—a reassuring thing to me.

Beth had grabbed the bull by the horns. Realizing she'd allowed herself to become too heavy, she did something about it. Her success came from her willingness to increase her level of exercise and eat better.

Not all overweight teens demonstrate this determination. But when they do, the outcome is usually very positive.

TEENS AND CALCIUM

Teenagers have special nutritional needs. You should discuss these with your health care professional, but for now I'd like to mention the importance of calcium.

The benefits of adequate calcium intake include decreased blood pressure, reduced risk for colon cancer and osteoporosis, and lower rates of obesity. Without adequate calcium in their diet, teens place themselves at risk for future osteoporosis—weakening of the bones. From roughly ages 9-18, the body creates a large percentage of its bone mass—up to 40 percent during 3-4 years of growth in adolescence.[1]

A recent report showed that only about 10 percent of girls and 30 percent of boys ages 12-19 receive the recommended amount of calcium.[2] Clearly we need to do better.

Past studies have suggested that children in this age range need 1200-1500 milligrams of calcium per day for optimal bone development.[3] But a study in the June 2004 issue of the *Journal of Pediatrics*[4] indicates that weight-bearing exercise may be as crucial as calcium intake in building children's bone mass.

Like muscles, bones must be used to reach peak strength. Kids can't just sit on the couch, drink milk, and hope they build strong bones. Physical activity must be part of the picture.

Dairy products are by far the best source of calcium for kids, and recent studies have shown that people drinking enough milk each day have an easier time losing weight or staying lean. Unfortunately, milk intake in children has fallen over the last 40-50 years; many children today drink more juice and pop than milk. Kids need to drink milk 3-4 times a day, in addition to eating other sources of calcium.

For kids who can't tolerate lactose, lactose-free 2 percent milk is readily available; calcium-fortified soymilk also provides about as much calcium as regular milk. Almonds are rich in calcium and an excellent snack or lunch staple for your adolescent. Other rich sources include broccoli, tofu, kale, beans, farina, Brazil nuts, sunflower seeds, and sardines. Compared to dairy, however, everything else pales when it comes to calcium content.

If your teenager doesn't ingest at least 1200 milligrams of calcium a day, ask your doctor whether you should consider a calcium supplement. It can be tough to stick to a daily regimen of pill-taking, though, and sometimes teens are lulled into a false sense of security if they're taking calcium tablets. The best solution is still to eat as many calcium-rich foods as possible, and to exercise regularly.

THE VITAMIN D DILEMMA

No matter how much calcium your teenager consumes, it won't help if it's not absorbed.

Vitamin D is essential to absorbing calcium in the gut; it's also linked to calcium and phosphorus metabolism. Since our bodies can produce it, it's not technically a vitamin. But we'll stick to convention and call it one.

Kids must either ingest enough vitamin D or be exposed to enough sunshine to allow their bodies to make it. Sunshine on the skin helps the body to manufacture vitamin D. Vitamin D deficiency, though relatively rare, is seen mainly in children with limited sun exposure, those with darker skin, or babies exclusively breast-fed for extensive periods without vitamin D supplementation. It's recommended that these groups of children receive extra vitamin D.

Sunscreen blocks the production of vitamin D in the skin. I'm acutely aware of the current guidelines stating that children should never go into the sun without sunscreen. If all children received enough dietary vitamin D, the issue might be moot; ideally, every youngster would drink plenty of vitamin D fortified milk and always apply sunscreen before going outside. But rarely do we see "ideal" in medicine.

At the risk of inviting the ire of my dermatology colleagues, I suggest a dose of pragmatism. First of all, we need to take skin type into account. If your child has fair skin, or you have a family history of skin cancer, be diligent about always using sunscreen. Be sure your child gets enough dietary vitamin D.

If, however, your child has darker skin, his risk of skin cancer is lower and his risk of vitamin D deficiency higher. If you live in a sunny climate or at high altitude, be vigilant about sun exposure protection; your child will receive a relatively high cumulative dose of sunshine over the course of his life.

If, like me, you live in a temperate zone where we seldom feel the sun from November to March, sunscreen application will be most important from April to October, between 10 A.M. and 4 P.M. Brief sun exposure at other times is unlikely to significantly increase your child's risk of skin cancer. Ask your physician whether he or she believes this effort to balance vitamin D and calcium metabolism with skin protection applies to you.

The question of how much sun exposure is wise will take more research to answer. Consider a study from the *British Medical Journal* in 2003.[5] It concluded, "[Higher] sun exposure in childhood and early adolescence is associated with a reduced risk of multiple sclerosis." It seems that sun exposure may dampen the activity of a cell which, in persons with multiple sclerosis, attacks myelin, a component of nervous tissue—resulting in the classic neurological disabilities of MS. This could account for the significantly higher prevalence of MS in northern climates than in warmer ones.

Don't throw away your sunscreen. For the sake of overall fitness, though, let your children play outside as much as they want—and use sunscreen as I've just described. As usual, moderation seems to be the better part of wisdom.

FAST FOOD AND SLOW COOKING

In our culture, fast food will always be part of most teenagers' lives. Instead of becoming obsessed with eliminating burgers and fries, accept their existence.

Still, you may be able to steer your teen to healthier fast food choices by eating out occasionally as a family at a chain that majors in more nutritious fare. You can request that allowance money not go toward fast food, because meals are available at home. Restaurant outings can be handled in a way that I'll discuss in an upcoming chapter.

The teen years are an especially good time to involve your child in meal planning and preparation. You can have younger kids in the kitchen regularly to help them get comfortable with the idea, but it's not until adolescence that most children really can pitch in.

Teens who plan and cook meals will be much more likely to eat them. They'll also appreciate the effort that goes into a meal and be more apt to learn about its components.

NEVER LET THEM SEE YOU SWEAT

No one would describe the teenage years as boring.

Never again will you be presented with such an opportunity to be a solid role model for your son or daughter every day. Never again will you experience such wonderful highs and discouraging lows. Here's hoping the former will greatly outnumber the latter.

Kids have a way of humbling parents, and this is especially true of teenagers. We moms and dads are wise, experienced, patient, loving . . . So why won't our kids listen to us? Why are we often so powerless to get through to them?

Since my wife and I are both in medicine, we tend to have a lot of conversations on medical topics—including nutrition and healthful behaviors. So when our girls got older, we were often discouraged to see them seemingly disregard our astute advice.

Remember that kids feed on parental angst. It's like blood in the water to a shark. Sometimes we just have to bite our tongues and not say anything. Appearing cool and collected, even when exasperated, is one of our best defenses.

Teach by example. Usually (though not always), as your kids get older your wisdom will be appreciated. Even on the subjects of nutrition and fitness.

Pray hard for your student's wisdom and patience—and for your own. The more you do, the more likely it is that you'll see the fruit of this principle: "The righteous man walks in his integrity; his children are blessed after him" (Proverbs 20:7).

PART SIX

CHANGING YOUR CHILD'S LIFESTYLE

CHAPTER TWELVE

SETTING REASONABLE GOALS

If you have to swallow a frog, try not to think about it.
If you have to swallow two frogs, don't swallow the smaller one first.
—IRISH PROVERB[1]

I t's time to start thinking about how your child's lifestyle might need to change in order to prevent or overcome obesity. That can be a little intimidating. In fact, you may be looking down at your proverbial parental plate and seeing a frog or two.

As the Irish proverb suggests, you shouldn't mull this situation over for very long. Let's get started!

WHERE ARE YOU GOING?

Setting goals is extremely important. If you have no target, where do you aim?

Children often respond very positively to simple goals. Knowing where you want your child's weight and fitness to be in one, two, or three years can be vital to success.

Keep in mind that we're undertaking a *long-term* strategy of lifestyle change. I consider 3-6 months to be the short term, with the long term being years.

I'll show you an easy way to determine how much weight your child needs to lose to achieve a healthier body mass index. Once you pick a one-year target weight, simply divide the amount your child needs to lose by 12 to show the monthly weight loss necessary.

As you monitor your child's weight, remember that weighing in more often than monthly can be counterproductive. Normal fluctuations due to fluid balance variations can trick you into thinking your child is losing too little or too much. As with measuring growth in children, you must consider a significant span of time.

To determine how much your child needs to lose to arrive at a certain BMI, use my "Desired BMI" formula that follows, an algebraic manipulation of the BMI equation.

Two adjustments must be made to the BMI formula when we use it to set a goal weight. First, to compensate for the growth of a child over the next year, we need to *add 2.5 inches to his or her present height.* Failing to do this will result in unnecessarily low goal weights, which could lead to discouragement and unreasonable expectations.

Second, we must use the goal BMI values for a child *one year older* than your child. These two adjustments will give us the goal weight for the child in one year.

You can use individually tailored variations of the formula, too. For instance, if your child has been growing at a constant rate of 2 inches per year over the past several years, use 2 in the equation that follows instead of 2.5.

Desired BMI formula:

Goal Weight = (desired BMI in 1 year) x (present height + 2.5) x (present height + 2.5)

JANE'S EXAMPLE

Here's an illustration of how this formula can be used with a young lady we'll call Jane.

Jane, 8, has a BMI of 21—greater than the 95th percentile for her age. Her height is 52 inches, about the 75th percentile for her age, and she weighs 80.77 pounds. Her physical exam is normal.

Jane's parents decide to help her embark on a program of weight loss and fitness. While improving her diet and getting her started with walking, they set goals for the coming year. They'd like her to lose enough weight to get from the 95th to the 85th percentile over the next 12 months.

Using the "Desired BMI" formula, and obtaining the BMI from the chart in Chapter 8, we can calculate Jane's goal weight:

$$\text{Goal Weight} = \frac{(19.1) \times (52+2.5) \times (52+2.5)}{703}$$

Note that 19.1 represents the 85th percentile BMI for a *9-year-old*—how old Jane will be *in a year.*

Jane's goal weight in one year is 80.7 pounds. Assuming she grows normally, all she needs to do is stay the same weight over the next year to move from the 95th to the 85th percentile BMI.

Realizing this, Jane's parents decide to be a bit more aggressive. The new goal: to move her to the 75th percentile in one year. To calculate her goal weight now, we can use the following figures:

$$\text{Goal Weight} = \frac{(18.0) \times (52+2.5) \times (52+2.5)}{703}$$

Jane's goal weight in one year for the 75th percentile is 76 pounds. Jane need only lose about 4.5 pounds over the next year to reach her goal.

From this exercise, it should be apparent that if you simply help your child to *stop gaining weight*, his or her BMI will slowly fall into an acceptable range.

Jane's example demonstrates how you can determine the weight your child needs to lose to move him or her into a healthier BMI percentile. Goals tend to be easy to set and more difficult to reach, but that doesn't diminish their importance. Once a goal is achieved, immediately set a new one and keep going.

If you prefer not to deal with numbers, your doctor can help you determine your child's most healthful weight.

THE POWER TO CHANGE

So far, our discussion has assumed that family and child are willing to proceed with changes. No amount of planning can replace the *desire* of a person or family to become more fit.

I remember seeing a boy who was about 20 pounds overweight for his height. His BMI was near the 97th percentile; he was unmistakably obese.

As I talked with him and his mom, it became obvious that she disagreed with me regarding their need to make changes. She was in denial, telling me she'd known many boys who were overweight and then "grew out of it, once they got rid of their baby fat."

It was apparent to me that if I pushed the issue, I would simply alienate the family. All I could do was clearly state my concerns and the possible long-term problems associated with obesity.

It was up to this family to decide to change things. I left the door open for the mom to call or meet with me again.

About six months later, mom called—asking for more information on obesity. I lost the family to follow-up, but I hope this young man is doing well.

As in so many areas, you can lead a horse to water . . . but you can't make him drink.

WHAT'S MY MOTIVATION?

If you're ready and willing to embark on changes, but your child isn't, how can you motivate him or her?

Most children wish to please their parents—at least when they're young. If your child fits that description, you can try to encourage him or her with extra hugs and kisses.

Whether or not that would be an incentive for your child, remember that the first thing to do is tell him the truth. If your child is old enough to understand, calmly and without drama explain the problems linked to being obese.

Since children tend to live in the present tense, yours are unlikely to comprehend completely. They'll relate more readily to present social difficulties like being teased or being chosen last on teams, and to current physical problems like fatigue or slowness in running, than they will to a longer-term threat like diabetes or heart disease.

Always be non-judgmental and gracious. Lead by example, both in physical activity and diet.

Small, creatively written contracts can help, serving as reminders of the agreement you've made. Kids like clear instructions. For instance, you might write, "We—Dad and Steve, members of the Smith family—wishing to increase our healthiness, agree to go for a walk together at least 5 nights a week, for at least 30 minutes each, for the next one month. This contract will be renewed each month unless both parties agree to end it. [You can add rewards and incentives here]."

Sign the agreement and put it on the refrigerator. Specify extra rewards available if the child does more than agreed upon. As the months go by, amend the contract together to add more activities or other expectations.

Another way to motivate your child is by running a contest. The two of you might compete by keeping track of the total number of sit-ups or push-ups done, or how long you walk, over the course of a month.

What about competition between two overweight siblings, to see how many pounds they can lose? Be careful here. If they tend to get along well and help each other, this might aid them in reaching their goals. But if rivalry between the two already exists, it may be best to avoid competition—so as not to discourage the child who ends up on the "short end."

GOING FOR THE GOAL

Now that you have a goal, how do you get there? What should you actually *do* to help your child lose weight?

In the next chapter you'll discover ways to get your child moving, increasing his or her Total Daily Energy Expenditure. After that, we'll deal with decreasing food intake.

CHAPTER THIRTEEN

GETTING YOUR CHILD MOVING

Let's be honest: Boosting your youngster's activity level may not be easy. How do you provide momentum for a child who's moving at the speed of molasses in January? How do you motivate a child who hates going outdoors and isn't used to physical activity?

I don't have no-miss answers to these questions—just no-gimmick ones. You'll find some suggestions on this subject—but in the end, you know your children better than anyone else. You know what will encourage them.

I hope that after reading this chapter (and Chapter 18, which describes activity boosters you might use), you'll know where you need to go and how to get there. The route you take will be up to you—and will vary considerably from family to family. Rarely in medicine is there only one means to an end, and fitness is no exception.

WHY ACTION FIGURES

Long-lasting weight control and fitness aren't likely without increased activity. It's possible to lose weight by diet alone, but that won't help your fitness level.

Dieting by itself is a recipe for frustration and heartbreak. Well-meaning parents who simply place their children on "diets" set themselves up for failure and worse. Kids soon learn that the "diet" is not helping and begin to lose heart, eventually becoming resigned to their present state.

Those who incorporate exercise into their fitness programs stand a much better chance for positive, long-term results. Regular exercisers, even if they don't lose weight, reduce their risk for some obesity complications.

Your goal shouldn't be weight loss alone, but improving your child's overall fitness and health. Among the benefits: fewer obesity-related dangers, and greater strength, endurance, flexibility, and confidence.

The most important thing to keep in mind is that this isn't a temporary, stopgap measure. It's a change in your family's lifestyle, and it must continue indefinitely. It isn't something you do until your child loses a specified amount of weight, only to return to old habits.

Most kids who lose weight and "fall off the wagon" go back to their prior lifestyle. They need refocusing. As with the alignment of your car, you need to make a correction when your child begins to drift off course.

If you're unwilling to maintain these changes, you should thoughtfully consider not wasting your child's time. I'm not trying to be unduly blunt, just truthful.

I assume, though, that if you've come this far, you're serious about helping your child.

Most people who lose weight regain much or all of it in the following year. We all know relatives and friends who've experienced temporary success with the latest diet fad, only to revert to their prior weight—or constantly vacillate. This ping-pong pattern may be harmful as well as discouraging, and isn't acceptable for our children.

Remember what we're aiming for: a gradual increase in Total Daily

Energy Expenditure, along with decreasing intake. This eliminates the seesaw phenomenon.

Simple? Yes.

Easy? Not always.

FITTING IN FITNESS

Say the word "exercise," and in grand Pavlovian style many will recoil with visions of dripping sweat, aching muscles, and smelly gymnasiums. Others may rebel against shiny health clubs with row upon row of machines and patrons who resemble models.

Whatever your initial reaction, try not to prejudge. For one thing, your child can improve his or her health dramatically and begin to lose weight without any of the above.

While your child may not be ready to run on the cross-country team without spending significant time training, just walking for 30 to 40 minutes each day can get him or her off the sedentary train. Recent studies suggest you can break a single block of activity into smaller pieces; for instance, a person can walk for 15 to 20 minutes twice a day and get the results of a 30- to 40-minute walk.

Since busyness may be your biggest barrier on the road to fitness, this is an important fact. Use it to your advantage! If you can't take a long walk with your child, break it up into smaller amounts.

For optimal fitness, your children should eventually participate in at least 60 minutes per day of moderate to vigorous exercise.[1] This shouldn't all be done in "organized" or parentally guided activities; kids should be sent out to run around and play as much as possible.

Where can you find time for daily exercise? If your child is like most in our culture these days, you'll find plenty of spare minutes by placing limits on the time your child watches television, plays video games, or surfs the Internet. Generally speaking, no more than a total of two hours a day should be spent on all these activities during the summer, and an hour or less per day during the school year.

If you don't impose these limits, your child will run out of time in short order due to homework and other commitments. The older kids are, the harder it is to cut back—so start these limits when they're young. If these simple restrictions commence before children know what they're missing, they're less likely to miss it.

The physical activity should be done as soon as your child gets home from school, or when you get home—but before dinner. Keep it fun and relaxed. Incentives may not be necessary; if they are, avoid food as a reward. Better encouragements would be extra time participating in a favorite hobby at home, or credits toward the purchase of some fun home exercise equipment such as a punching bag, speed rope, or free weights.

TAKE A HIKE

The easiest way to get your child moving is to start walking each day. Some would say three to five times a week is sufficient, and it may be. But I want to get you into a routine of *daily* exercise. By doing so, you'll feel less guilty if your child misses a day—and results will be achieved more quickly.

Begin by walking 15 minutes in one direction and returning. Walk briskly, maintaining an upright posture, concentrating on contracting your abdominal muscles. Walking together is a wonderful way to spend time with your children and make a real difference in their health.

If you can't walk for 30 minutes on a particular day, do whatever you can. You can walk for a longer period the next day. As you develop a routine, begin to lengthen your walks a bit, especially in better weather. Increase by about five or ten minutes every week or two; you should find this gradual change quite manageable.

Realize that when I say "walking" with your children, I mean *you* will be walking while *they* run, skip, explore, walk, and run some more. Ever noticed kids on the deck of a pool? It's as if their bodies don't know how to walk—just skitter and run. A stern reprimand from a lifeguard only brings a two-second slowing of their pace.

The benefits of walking are hard to overstate. Thomas Jefferson, writing to Peter Carr on August 10, 1787, stated quite presciently, "Take a great deal of exercise and on foot. Of all exercises walking is the best. [Riding] a horse gives but a kind of half exercise, and a carriage is no better than a cradle. No one knows, till he tries, how easily a habit of walking is acquired. A person who never walked three miles will in the course of a month be able to walk fifteen or twenty without fatigue. I have known some great walkers, and had particular accounts of many more; and I never knew or heard of one who was not healthy or long lived. Love of repose will lead, in its progress, to a suspension of healthy exercise, a relaxation of mind, an indifference to everything around you, and finally to a debility of body, hebetude [dullness] of mind, the farthest of all things from happiness."[2]

Well stated!

BEYOND WALKING

Other aerobic activities you can add to your routine include bicycling, rollerblading, swimming, and jumping rope (see Appendix C for the calories burned by each of these). Younger children especially love jumping rope; accompanied by a suitable song, they'll continue for a long time.

In the summer, keep up your walking program even if your child spends the rest of the day at the pool. In winter, or bad weather, many kids would enjoy a foot-activated video game such as *Dance Dance Revolution*.

Whatever you pick, build up slowly and stay with it. It's essential that children enjoy the activity, so allow them to choose as much as possible. They may resist at first, especially if they're quite overweight; it may be physically taxing for them to walk longer than a few minutes.

Exercise has a way of becoming habit-forming. After a while you'll notice that if you miss a few days, you won't feel as well. This is because endorphins, the body chemicals produced during exercise, make you feel good—and because of the mental benefits of aerobic activity. Kids tell me all the time that they feel better when they've been exercising regularly.

That was the case with a young man named Mike, who came to see me a few years ago. He had no medical problems, but was just a smidgen heavy with a BMI at the 84th percentile. A year later he'd gained an excessive amount; by age 12 he was 56 inches tall and 102 pounds. There were no signs of a hormonal imbalance.

We instituted some simple changes in his diet and routines—nothing dramatic, just common sense. His mom and dad were very helpful; Mom got the entire family eating more wholesome foods, and Dad got Mike out playing ball and running.

After he'd been more active for a while, Mike told me it made him feel "happy with life"; if he missed a few days, he didn't feel as good. This is typical of exercise's effect.

A year later Mike had lost two pounds and grown two inches. His BMI had gone from 22.9 (about the 92nd percentile) to 20.9 (about the 83rd percentile). Mom noticed that his clothes fit better, and he was thrilled when he saw the numbers.

By age 13, Mike was up to 60.5 inches; his weight stayed at 100 pounds, for a BMI of 19.2—less than the 75th percentile.

Mike says he feels great. He's become a faster, stronger, better baseball player. He didn't do anything dramatic; he just made a few changes on each side of the energy equation.

You can do the same. So start moving with your kids!

MUSCLE YOUR WAY TO FITNESS

As you advance in activities and time spent on them, try adding some strength training.

Remember BMR (Basal Metabolic Rate)? If not, look over Chapter 3 to refresh your memory. Strength training, also called resistance training, is an excellent way to increase BMR. That increases Total Daily Energy Expenditure (TDEE), because muscle needs quite a bit of energy to maintain itself. Resistance training also can strengthen bones by helping to build and maintain bone mass. That's very important for preventing osteoporosis in later years.

Children can begin strength training at any age. Based on research, the American Academy of Pediatrics published a policy statement in 2001 outlining the benefits and risks of weight training in children.[3]

The advantages of strength training include protection from joint injury, improved sports performance, greater confidence, and possibly increased BMR. Why "possibly"? Because increases in BMR are not as substantial in preadolescent children due to a lack of testosterone, a hormone necessary for building muscle mass. Strength will rise, however, as muscles learn to fire more effectively. Injuries rarely occur with this kind of exercise, and should be nonexistent if safety recommendations are carefully followed.

Remember, we're not talking about *power* lifting. That type of training, designed to build large muscle mass, should not be considered until a student is physically mature.

The key to safe strength training in children is using proper technique through a full range of motion, favoring the number of repetitions over the amount of weight. Two sets of 12-15 repetitions are ideal. If your child can't do these fairly easily, reduce the weight. Start with an amount he or she can handle easily; then work up slowly.

If you don't have access to free weights, try push-ups, chin-ups, sit-ups, back-ups, and lunges. These exercises can be done by a child of almost any age. I'll review specific exercises, stretches, and workout plans in Chapter 19.

Even if you have free weights available, the aforementioned exercises are highly recommended for strengthening the entire body—especially your "core"—rather than isolating a single area. Core muscle groups include your abdominal, back, hip, and gluteus (buttocks) muscles, and are extremely important in balancing and stabilizing your body. Everyone—especially athletes—can benefit from a strengthened core.

Challenge your kids to slowly improve and get stronger. See how many repetitions they can do at first; chart their progress to encourage them and keep them motivated. Offer rewards: a movie with mom and dad for a certain level of achievement, a piece of sports equipment or tickets to a ball game for another. You may want to enter exercise data into a computer spreadsheet program to show your kids their progress graphically.

Always warm up prior to your exercise session with low-impact movements like walking, arm circles, and lifting your knees to your chest repeatedly. This will get your heart pumping and your blood flowing, warming up your muscles—thus reducing the risk of injury to muscles and joints.

Teach your child the importance of proper breathing during exercise. Inhale on the passive half; exhale during the dynamic phase, when you exert power. For example, during a push-up, exhale as you push up and inhale while slowly lowering. Correct breathing enhances oxygen delivery to working muscles, resulting in less fatigue.

Repetitions should always be done in a smooth, controlled manner. Working on balance while resistance training is also very important. For instance, you can stand on one leg while doing arm curls or a military press, or do push-ups while your feet are on an exercise ball.

Some exercises will be difficult for your kids at first. Few overweight children will be able to do a chin-up; they may need a little help, but most kids love a challenge if they feel encouraged rather than judged. Many younger ones are used to swinging on the "monkey bars" anyway.

Engage in strength training "play" with your child. Ongoing competition is often a good idea. Most kids will love it, especially if you let them win every now and then; it's even better if they beat you outright. I believe it's okay for siblings, too, to compete against each other in physical activities—as long as you make sure it doesn't become contentious. Most children are naturally competitive; life is, too, so you might as well allow them to practice in the context and protection of your family.

Strength training should be done three to four times a week, with a day of rest between sessions to allow muscle tissue to recover. Training more than four times a week can be detrimental.

Start with a set of eight to twelve repetitions of each exercise. Work up to two sets of twelve to fifteen as your child becomes stronger. If this proves too easy for the child, you can slow down the exercise. Performing a resistance exercise in a slow, deliberate way greatly increases the difficulty. If you doubt this, try doing a few push-ups—taking five to six seconds to push up, then five to six seconds to lower. See how much harder it is than doing them quickly.

Some muscle soreness is normal, especially when starting out. But joint pain or swelling isn't, and needs to be evaluated by a physician.

Muscle soreness, which will diminish over a few days and as your child becomes more fit, shouldn't prevent continuing.

Keep in mind that strength is much more useful when accompanied by flexibility. Aerobic (walking, running, swimming), strength (weight lifting), and flexibility (stretching) training are the three building blocks of fitness. Children are naturally flexible, but you should always incorporate some stretching into their routine—especially after resistance training.

MORE GOOD HABITS

There are many other ways to increase TDEE. One is "taking the long road"; another is getting involved in competitive sports.

Sometimes the shortest route between two points isn't the healthiest one. When you visit the mall or grocery store, park further from the entrance and take a walk. Use stairs whenever possible, avoiding elevators and escalators. If you can, have your children walk to school; accompany them if they're younger.

Resist playing chauffeur if it's safe for your children to walk or ride their bicycles. Play outside with your kids regularly, running around as much as you can. These things may seem insignificant by themselves, but they add up.

Competitive sports are excellent for children who want to participate. Most kids love playing baseball, basketball, football, or soccer, and these can be fantastic sources of exercise. But if you find that after some loving encouragement your child doesn't wish to sign up, try waiting another year and then offering the opportunity again. In the meantime, you can keep your child moving at home without having to join a team.

If your child does play, emphasize the sportsmanship aspect of competition. Teach your child to play hard but fairly, always respecting his or her opponent.

If you do get involved in team sports, be careful not to cancel out the benefits with high-calorie snacks and drinks. Avoid a routine of ice cream or other goodies after each game; occasional treats are fine. Some teams supply soft drinks or Gatorade after each practice or game; opt for water whenever possible, or a diet soft drink.

Beverages like Gatorade are rarely needed for children if they're drinking enough water. In very hot climates or with high humidity, if children perspire excessively, a fluid and electrolyte replacement drink such as Gatorade may be appropriate. Water is by far the most important thing a child should drink when exercising—taking frequent, small drinks of cool water to maintain hydration.

SPORTS FOR A LIFETIME

Want to help your child avoid obesity in the future as well as the present? Involving him in an active hobby like tennis or golf can be a continuing source of fitness as well as fun and confidence.

These are literally sports for a lifetime. If your child develops an interest and really enjoys playing, he'll spend less time on TV or some other less beneficial pursuit. The whole family can enjoy these activities together, and the skills gained can open social and business doors in the future.

When playing golf, make sure your child always walks; save cart riding for special occasions. Try an inexpensive course that lends itself to learning. Let your younger players whack a few old golf balls into the ponds—they'll love it.

Golf used to be viewed as a "non-athletic" sport, but conditioning and strength training are now an integral part of the game—

thanks mostly to the influence of Gary Player and Tiger Woods. As an avid golfer, I can testify to the fact that walking 18 holes is good exercise. You'll end up walking four to five miles over the course of the round—maybe longer if you're, shall we say, a novice.

Tennis is another wonderful sport to play with your kids. Two racquets, a can of balls, a court in a park, and you're ready to go! A healthy person can play for nearly his or her entire life, and it's a prime source of exercise. Doctors are starting to appreciate some of the longevity-supporting benefits of active hobbies, too.

Some of my fondest childhood memories are of playing tennis and golf with my mom, dad, and friends. The municipal course where I learned to golf is still a welcome haven for me from the stresses of life.

So find an activity your family likes to do, and get to it. Don't stare at that "frog" and wait or make excuses. The time to begin is now!

CHAPTER FOURTEEN

DIET–A FOUR-LETTER WORD

I n the Bible, dietary recommendations changed through the ages. Current recommendations are found in Acts 10:9-16 and 1 Timothy 4:3-5.

As those passages teach, we have the freedom to eat all kinds of foods. But this doesn't mean you should go out and feed your kids anything and everything.

I believe part of our charge to subdue the earth (Genesis 1:28) includes using scientific knowledge to improve people's lives and glorify God. Having learned a lot about nutrition and human physiology, we know that some things are better for us than others. In our effort to prevent and overcome obesity, we should use that God-given knowledge.

Remember, though, that this isn't about getting children to look "ideal," or to keep their weight from "embarrassing" us. We want to help our children reach optimal weight and fitness so that they can stay healthy—in order to serve God to the best of their abilities, thus leading happy and productive lives.

OUT WITH THE BAD, IN WITH THE GOOD

This may be the toughest of your lifestyle changes. For many children *and* adults, "diet" is a four-letter word.

But we're *not* going to place your child on a diet, per se. The plan is to eliminate the worst foods, substitute better ones, and present them in smaller portions. By eating a bit less and more slowly, and consuming only occasional snacks with low glycemic indices, your kids can experience slow, gradual metabolic change.

They won't be fighting hunger pangs or cravings due to a lack of calories or in reaction to insulin surges. Any meal plan that leaves a child feeling hungry much of the time is doomed to failure. Eventually cravings drive them to binge—destroying what we're trying to accomplish.

Adults are the same way, of course. People in our culture tend to eat way too much; overindulgence is the main cause of obesity, and the problem is slowly metastasizing to the rest of the Western world. Gluttony is a serious matter, as Proverbs 23:21 indicates: "For the drunkard and the glutton will come to poverty, and drowsiness will clothe a man with rags."

I once saw a rotund doctor lecturing quite expertly and with passion on alcoholism. I appreciated his doing so. But the thought crossed my mind as I watched him that some people are killing themselves with the bottle, others with the fork. Our economy offers an abundance of food at reasonable prices, but this has become a double-edged sword. Somewhere along the way we lost our willpower to forgo the excess.

Our collective eating routines have influenced our children. How can we expect kids to change if we don't?

As you guide your kids toward more modest portions, consider joining them. If you do this correctly, neither of you will mind—and your kids may not even notice. This is why I say we're not going to place them on a "diet."

In fact, dieting may be counterproductive. When a person loses weight on a "diet" and gains it back, she not only suffers a psychological setback; it becomes harder to lose weight over the long haul. A study of adolescents showed that those who placed themselves on restrictive diets actually gained more weight over a three-year period than their non-dieting peers did![1]

One of the keys to long-term health and longevity is simply eating less. Benjamin Franklin realized this when he said, "To lengthen thy life, lessen thy meals." Our bodies can thrive on significantly less food than we now shovel into them. Quality, not quantity, should be our motto. The key is making certain that we offer our children only the best, most efficient fuel possible.

TIME IS ON YOUR SIDE

To successfully change your child's eating lifestyle, we need to design a pragmatic program that is easy to follow, tasty, and satisfying; allows for choices; and is introduced in such a way that your child fails to notice a big change. It *is* possible!

Remember, though, that it took time for the extra weight to accumulate. It will take time for your child to lose it. Fortunately, children don't have to lose weight to thin out; because they're growing, BMI will fall even if their weight stays the same.

Take, for example, a fictitious boy of 4 who weighs 60 pounds and is 40 inches tall. His BMI of 26.4 indicates he is seriously obese. Assuming he grows about 2.5 inches a year over the next 3 years, and if his weight stays at 60 pounds, his BMI will fall to 23.4 by age 5, 20.8 by age 6, and 18.7 by age 7.

This gradual, no-gimmick approach requires patience of all

involved. But it doesn't require superhuman effort. Sudden, quick weight loss isn't necessary to move a child toward a healthier weight.

I recently saw a young boy who'd accomplished exactly that. He'd gone from 47 to 63 pounds in a year from ages 4 to 5, due to excess snacking and junk food. His BMI was 20, well above the 95th percentile. No-gimmick counseling and a motivated family led to cutting out many of the unwholesome foods and exercising more.

This year, at age 6, he's 3 inches taller and the same weight. Though he didn't lose an ounce, he looks much better; his BMI has fallen to 17.9. His dad said frankly, "He doesn't have a big gut anymore." His family needs to avoid resting on its laurels and continue the positive changes.

Most children halt extra weight gain once they stop eating junk food, temper a bit the amount they eat, and begin to get moving. They, like your child, should aim for gradual weight loss that reaches the 75th percentile BMI (or under) in a year or two—which puts them safely below the level at which health risks increase.

If you and your child are excited about that improvement, you may wish to continue to lose gradually under the care of your doctor. By continuing to eat a healthful diet and maintaining daily exercise, your child should be able to stay fit and trim indefinitely.

HOW MUCH SHOULD THEY EAT?

Should kids count calories? I believe that's largely a waste of time. Most children know only whether they're satisfied, regardless of the numbers. They couldn't care less whether they're eating 800, 1200, or 2400 calories per day.

Let their bodies tell them how much to eat. Remember, they have a fantastic internal mechanism for that purpose—as long as we don't mess it up by letting them eat too quickly or consume too many foods with high glycemic loads that cause insulin surges and subsequent hunger. By eating more fiber, fewer high-glycemic-index foods, and less added sugar, they can "reset" their hunger mechanisms back to normal. Then they can work on becoming fit via exercise. Just as overeating can be learned, it can be unlearned.

Having said that, it's still worth noting basic guidelines for children's caloric intake (see Appendix D).[2] The problem with these numbers is that a child's size and Total Daily Energy Expenditure make a big difference—and aren't accounted for. The taller and more muscular and more active a child, the more calories he needs.

So view these guidelines with caution. If your weight loss efforts hit a roadblock, consult a nutrition professional to help you fine-tune your child's intake. Caloric needs can also be assessed by measuring a person's Basal Metabolic Rate (BMR)—which can now be gauged with a breath test. Many health clubs offer this service as part of a comprehensive approach to weight loss and fitness.

The idea of lowering food intake raises the anxiety level in some parents. They fear their children already don't eat as well as they should. But I've found that children described as having a "poor" appetite, or as "poor" eaters, are as healthy as those described as eating well. This observation was confirmed in a recent study[3] showing that "poor" eaters consumed as much as "good" ones. The growth and development of the two groups were the same.

I can't count the number of times parents have brought a child in for a checkup and told me that their youngster eats absolutely nothing. When I show them that she's gained two pounds over the past few months, they often look at me as if I'm kidding.

One mom wanted me to reweigh her child because she was sure the first reading was wrong. How, she asked, could a child gain weight on a "diet of air"? The first weight was confirmed. Now this mom and I joke, as her kids continue to grow, that they must be on the "air diet."

If you lead a horse to water, don't worry—he'll drink if he's thirsty. Offer your kids healthy foods, and their bodies will take it from there.

WHAT ABOUT WEIGHT CONTROL PROGRAMS?

If you and your child find it tough to stick to the dietary recommendations in this book, one option to consider is joining a program such as Weight Watchers or Jenny Craig.

I mention these two because they're among the most popular and successful. The long-term track record of Weight Watchers is hard to beat. For 40 years people have been losing weight with this program—provided they stayed with it.

One advantage of Weight Watchers is its realistic view of how people behave when they decide to lose weight. People don't want to give up all their favorite foods—and when push comes to shove, they won't. By assigning point values to foods and the amounts to be eaten, the program helps people control intake while letting them eat some of their favorites.

The participant is allowed only so many "points" per day. The net effect is that less is eaten, resulting in gradual weight loss. This emphasis on gradual improvement shows an understanding of the risks of rapid weight loss, and that the true aim is lasting behavioral change. Because a variety of foods are consumed, deficiencies in the diet are very rare, and the program tends to be well accepted.

Children age 10 and above can participate. I've written many "prescriptions" for kids to accompany their parents to Weight Watchers. The program is definitely more effective if multiple family members participate; they motivate and watch each other. As for children under 10, they shouldn't have to use such a program; their parents need to provide that leadership.

Jen is one person who's discovered the value of a structured program. Her parents began to worry a few years ago as they saw her overeat and gain weight rapidly. Dad sensed she was resorting to food for comfort.

Jen began to hear kids comment on her being "fat." Her parents' hearts broke as they saw her hurting. Her mom worried that Jen wouldn't be treated fairly, that she wouldn't have any dates when she got older, and that she'd have trouble keeping up in sports.

For Jen, several realities began to settle in. She knew that if she continued being overweight, she would "need blood tests"—and she was terrified of needles. And shopping for clothes got more difficult as things didn't fit correctly; baggy clothes became the norm.

She tried to "diet," but without success. Each weight gain brought more disappointment. Tension began to bubble up; family battles ensued.

After we talked with Jen and her mom about what strategy to take, they decided to give Weight Watchers a try.

Jen loved the structure and challenge of the program; she used her considerable math skills to calculate points. Best of all, she saw results almost immediately. Her first goal was to fit into a pair of jeans she'd sized out of—and she did it. Shopping for clothes was fun again, and her self-confidence returned. After taking part in Weight Watchers for about 25 weeks, this lovely young lady has lost 19 pounds.

Her mom told me two things have contributed especially to Jen's success. First, mom and dad didn't force her into the program; they encouraged her but let her take the initiative. Second, Jen is free to make some choices about what she eats. If she wants a couple of cookies after dinner, she eats less during the day to save up points. This feeling of self-determination can be especially vital for older kids. It also largely eliminates the tension between child and parent.

Jen may continue to battle excess weight in adulthood. But she's very happy with her success, and her parents are thrilled!

Then there's Susan. She comes from a heavy family. Her weight had been steadily increasing for years, despite counseling. At age 14 she was 63.5 inches tall and 209 pounds, for an extremely high BMI of 36.4. Feeling very tired and with pain in her knees, she got serious about normalizing her weight.

Susan and her mom had told me they knew she was sedentary and eating too much, but had lacked the motivation to change. Now they decided to enter Weight Watchers. A few of Susan's friends also decided to work out with her, and did so three or four times a week.

What a difference! Within 10 months Susan had grown an inch and lost 57 pounds, for a much-improved BMI of 25.7. Another 6 months saw an additional inch of growth, with her weight down to 149.5. Her BMI was now at 24.5, right at the 85th percentile.

Like Jen, Susan has relished being able to choose foods within the structure of the program. She's learned about wholesome eating habits and exercise—and put that knowledge to work, even influencing her two sisters positively. The smile on her face has been a priceless reminder of why I do what I do.

A structured program like Weight Watchers is one weapon to consider in the battle of the bulge you're helping your child wage. If you elect to use such a program, try to stick with the foods recommended in this book as much as possible.

What about camps for overweight children? These vary greatly, so ask your doctor for a recommendation. As you research options, keep the following thoughts in mind:

1. Camp can, and should, be a fun time for kids. Look for one that emphasizes physical activities—especially teaching new ones to children, so that when they return they'll know more ways to stay on the move.

2. Examine the camp's philosophy and policies. What are kids fed? What are they taught about eating? Are kids allowed to eat any-

thing as long as they limit portions? Are most junk foods not available? Does the camp support the fitness principles you've been trying to teach?

3. See if you can find a friend or two to join your child. Bringing your own support group fights loneliness, boosts acceptance, bolsters confidence, and increases the likelihood that the program will be effective.

If camps interest you, research them carefully. If you find a good fit, the experience can be a memorable one that reinforces the changes you're instituting at home.

CHAPTER FIFTEEN

HOW SHOULD WE THEN EAT?

Let's get down to brass tacks. I want to offer you some ideas about eating that you can apply immediately and continue indefinitely.

We'll begin with a dozen principles I call "The 12 Commandments of Eating." They summarize many of the no-gimmick tips I've offered so far. Even though I wouldn't engrave them on stone tablets, I'd suggest that following them will make a powerful and positive difference in your family's fitness.

THE 12 COMMANDMENTS OF EATING

1. Make a priority of eating together as a family. Do this for as many meals a day as possible. Schedules may make this difficult, but it pays handsome benefits in stronger relationships and healthier eating habits.

2. Make sure your children wake up early enough to eat an unhurried, healthy breakfast. This means getting to bed early enough to wake at the prescribed time, feeling well-rested. And that means plenty of daytime exercise to help ensure a proper bedtime.

3. Children should drink milk at each meal—2 percent (age one and over) or skim (age two and over). Several studies have shown that drinking milk with a meal decreases the total calories consumed.

Ovaltine added to milk may be your ace in the hole for a recalcitrant milk drinker; start with 100 percent Ovaltine-flavored milk, very gradually mixing in regular milk until the flavored milk is eliminated. Chocolate-flavored soymilk is another option if you can't get your kids to drink any milk.

4. Children should also drink water at each meal and have it available throughout the day. Adequate hydration is crucial to health, and water with meals may lead to an earlier feeling of fullness. Forget juices, sports drinks, and pop. If your child can't live without a flavored beverage, let him or her have an occasional diet soft drink or diet lemonade.

5. When serving meals, spread the food thinly over the plate, use smaller plates, or both. Not allowing different foods to touch also cuts down the amount on the plate. Use a shallow bowl that holds less volume. Your child's senses will be "tricked" into believing she's eaten more than she thinks, lessening the chance of overeating. Also, serve dinner in courses—starting with higher-volume foods like fruits and vegetables. Feeling satisfied is affected most by the *volume* of food, not the caloric density. Save higher-calorie dishes for the end, when your kids will be less hungry and probably will eat less of them.

6. Encourage your child to use proper manners and to chew his food quietly and thoroughly. This won't affect digestion, but will help your child eat more slowly—one key to avoiding overeating. Putting the fork or spoon down after every few bites can slow intake, too.

7. Cultivate conversation during each meal—and keep the TV off. If mouths are engaged in talk and manners are minded, food will be going in at a more leisurely pace—giving your stomachs a chance to communicate with your brains' hunger sensors.

8. Don't offer second helpings until at least 20 minutes after the start of a meal. This provides time for your children's brains to get the "I'm full" message. Don't serve seconds until everyone has finished first helpings; keep food on the stove instead of the table, thereby reducing the temptation to grab seconds too soon. Second helpings should be offered of "Birdie" or "Par" (see the next chapter) foods only.

9. Except where food allergies or other medical conditions are involved, don't serve your child custom-made meals different from those the rest of the family gets. Even if your child turns up his nose at a few of your meals, stay calm. His internal hunger drive ensures that he'll eat enough over time.

10. Try to avoid fast foods. If you decide to eat at such a chain, skip soft drinks, fries, and fried foods. Find eateries that offer sandwiches with whole-grain bread and more healthy choices. Insist that your kids drink milk and water with the meal.

11. Avoid deep-fried foods and refined sugar. The deep frying process adds loads of calories and heart-clogging trans fat. Sugar can trigger insulin surges. Using a sugar substitute like sucralose can reduce refined sugar intake.

12. Whenever possible, eat fresh fruits and vegetables and unprocessed, higher-fiber foods. Avoid "instant," "pre-made," "refined," and "bleached."

Many of life's greatest successes come from doing the "little things" well. These commandments—or suggestions—are designed to help you do just that. Some will be harder than others for you to follow, but try as many as you can.

TEN TIPS FOR PREP AND PORTIONS

How can you get kids to try new foods, eat proper portions, and take responsibility in the kitchen? Here are 10 ways.

1. Even though it's probably faster and easier for you to do all the food preparation, involve your children in this process. Start early in life. Teaching about food should be a hands-on experience, despite youthful tendencies to spill, burn, and drop things.

2. You don't always have to serve a salad, vegetable, and meat; think outside the box. Creative appetizers can make a meal. Or eat Spanish *tapas* style—offering small tastes of a variety of things.

3. Eating smaller amounts over a longer period can be more fun. It also can lead to eating less. How about a "progressive dinner," in which you move from room to room or house to house for successive courses? Or a hike or picnic that alternates food with physical activity?

4. Encourage school-age kids to find interesting recipes in magazines and books; then help them plan and prepare the food. Nothing motivates like pride of ownership. You could even have them research the meal's fiber, protein, and vitamin content.

5. Older teens can be encouraged to regularly plan, shop for, and prepare entire meals. Give them a budget and let them know your nutritional expectations.

6. Buy a small food scale to teach kids proper portion size. For instance, the pieces of chicken they've been eating may be 8-10 ounces. A 4-ounce serving would be more appropriate—the size of a deck of cards. Use a measuring cup to find out how much a serving of cereal really is.

7. If you make a new food, everyone should try a bite. That includes dad and mom.

8. Be creative in your search for healthful recipes. You'll find some in Chapter 17. Beyond that, consult cookbooks geared toward vegetarians and low-fat diets. While "low fat" is not necessarily good, you can glean many superb ideas from these sources—and from health magazines and the Internet. Look for recipes containing foods with

lower glycemic loads, containing more vegetables, legumes, whole grains, fruits, fish, and lean meat. If a recipe doesn't turn out as planned, have family members offer suggestions on how to improve it. Our family's three-bean chili recipe was perfected this way!

9. Presentation is important, so let kids help you set the table neatly and make the meal look appetizing. Smaller children can help by drawing place mats that you can laminate in plastic.

10. Once a month, have an international or regional cuisine weekend, where you plan and eat meals representing a distinct part of your country or the world. Southwest, Californian, Cajun, New England, Italian, Mediterranean, Mexican, Thai, Japanese, Chinese, British, Irish, German, Indian, Moroccan, and French foods are a sample of the possibilities. When our girls were younger, we occasionally planned meals with an international theme, tied to teaching geography. They would research other parts of the world—Norway, for instance—and prepare a meal common to that country.

EIGHT SIMPLE RULES ON DESSERTS, SNACKS, AND RESTAURANTS

For many kids as well as adults, the best-laid plans for good nutrition are sabotaged by sweets, treats, and going out to eat. It doesn't have to be that way, though. Consider the following thoughts.

1. If you want a dessert now and then, fine. Just eat smaller portions.

2. Fresh fruit makes the best dessert. Small chunks of dark chocolate can be an occasional indulgence. They're rich in antioxidants; a small amount can be very satisfying, yet fairly low in calories. My personal favorites are Dove brand "Promises" dark chocolate bites—about 40 calories for one.

3. I'm not a big fan of low-fat ice cream. Some kids and parents seem to think that because it's low-fat they can eat a lot more. Better to eat the good stuff every now and then, in small portions.

4. Snacking is often unnecessary if a child eats properly three times a day. Some contend that children have smaller stomachs, and thus need to eat more often; sure, their stomachs are smaller, but proportionately so! Do they *really* need to eat something every hour or two?

Often parents tell me, "I had to keep them occupied," when their children were eating crackers or drinking juice in my office. That's how children develop a habit of expecting to eat every few hours, hungry or not. If they're engaged in another activity, they'll usually make it through snack time without a hitch.

Try to break your children of the routine snack habit, and see how they do. If you find they do better with a snack between meals, keep it small and wholesome.

5. Don't give up on the idea of dining out as a family occasionally, even if staying home seems socially and nutritionally safer. Some of your most pleasurable and memorable times together could happen when you venture out to eat. I believe it's important to head out now and then so your kids can learn how to behave in social situations.

6. When you treat your family to a restaurant experience, enjoy yourself! Don't obsess about carbs and fatty acids while you study the menu. You can, however, limit the "damage" by avoiding pre-meal white bread and nixing fries and soft drinks. If possible, order fruit or vegetables in place of potatoes, chips, fries, or onion rings. Drink milk and water; share a salad and a dessert.

7. Lay out ground rules *before* you go to a restaurant, in order to avoid conflict there. Then try to keep the conversation lively, just as you would at home, to slow everyone's eating pace.

8. Remember that whether you're eating at home or dining out, mealtime is not the time to nag your children about how much they

eat. Simply enjoy the love and company of your family. As Proverbs 15:17 observes, "Better is a dinner of herbs where love is, than a fatted calf with hatred."

FOLLOWING THE RULES

Whether or not your child is overweight, I trust the suggestions in this chapter will nudge him or her—and your whole family—down the road toward fitness.

If after a few months of following these guidelines you find that your child is not losing excess weight or is still gaining, meet with a nutritionist or registered dietitian. He or she can help you assess your child's intake and identify unnecessary calories.

Use what you've learned so far about glycemic index, glycemic load, fiber, and other factors to make wise choices. Don't hesitate to try new things. A steady process of gradually lowering intake coupled with increasing exercise will eventually yield positive results.

One way to make wise choices is by using a "rating system" that ranks foods according to the good or harm they tend to do. The next chapter explains just such a system, and names some nutritional heroes and villains you need to know.

CHAPTER SIXTEEN

WHAT TO EAT—THE BIRDIE, PAR, AND BOGEY SYSTEM

Which foods are best for your child? Which should you leave on the supermarket shelf?

To help you plan your shopping and eating, I've placed common foods into three categories—from most wholesome to least healthful.

Since I'm fond of knocking a little white ball around, I've named the three lists "Birdie," "Par," and "Bogey." If you're not a golfer, you need to know that when you make a birdie it's a good thing; you've used one less stroke than the standard ("par") to hit the ball into the hole. "Par" is the standard score; you might call it "average." As for "bogey," think "bad"—it took you one more stroke than par to get the ball into the hole.

How do these labels apply to food? "Birdie" foods are those that are best for you; let your child eat as much as he wants every day, offering a good variety. "Par" foods are good, but should be enjoyed in moderation—several servings a week each, for breakfast, lunch, and dinner.

A "Bogey" rating identifies foods we should be eliminating from our diets. These foods can be eaten once in a while, but their negatives outweigh any positives. "Bogey" foods may be unavoidable at times, but limit them to an occasional indulgence.

DOES THE SYSTEM WORK?

A look at the lists may discourage you at first, especially if you doubt your child will eat any of the "Birdie" foods. Take heart: This is not an all-or-nothing proposition. Gradually incorporate more of the best foods and eliminate the worst ones.

Following this system will help you . . .

- reduce your child's intake of saturated fat and increase intake of healthy plant fat;
- reduce intake of sugar, high-glycemic-load foods, and processed foods;
- boost fruit and vegetable consumption;
- increase intake of whole grains, nuts, and legumes;
- add fiber; and
- provide a healthy variety, thus including all necessary nutrients.

My lists aren't exhaustive; other foods can be a part of a wholesome diet, too. Do your homework and add to the list as you see fit.

If many of the foods seem unfamiliar to you, maybe you haven't been eating very well. Remember the old TV commercial, "Try it, you'll like it"? Try eating better, and I think you'll like it. If your family can eat properly *most* of the time, you'll make headway.

Before you review the lists, remember that weight loss is less likely when you attempt to "diet." If you ban all your children's favorite foods, they may crave them all the more. The same is true of adults, which explains the failure of most restrictive diets.

The key isn't severe deprivation. It's that calorie intake must be less than Total Daily Energy Expenditure. Eat less than you burn, and you'll lose weight.

If your children are very young and have yet to be introduced to many unhealthy foods, this is your chance to offer them only the most wholesome foods on the list. You *can* mold their tastes. Give them foods with a large variety of colors, too; you'll automatically be giving them a good nutritional selection.

So here are my recommendations. If you have trouble following them, let your kids have some of their favorite foods now and then. Remember that bottom line: moderation.

BREAKFAST: BIRDIE FOODS

Birdie foods are worth eating every day. Here are some to wake up to:

- whole-grain, low-sugar, high-fiber (five grams or more per serving) cereals
- whole-grain toast with a "no trans fat" spread like Smart Balance; low- or no-sugar fruit jams or natural peanut butter
- non-instant oatmeal; add fruit or sucralose (Splenda) to sweeten
- apples, bananas, berries of all kinds, cherries (if you remove the pits first), grapefruit, grapes, kiwi, mango, oranges, peaches, pears, plums
- plain, unsweetened yogurt; add fruit or Splenda for natural sweetness
- two percent (age one and over) or skim milk (age two and over); water, caffeine-free jasmine or plain green tea, grapefruit juice

"But I thought you had a 'no fruit juice' rule," you might be saying. A small serving of fresh-squeezed, no-added-sugar, with-pulp grapefruit juice with breakfast is my one exception. It has a lower GL, and if eaten with other lower-GI foods should not interfere with what you're trying to accomplish.

This isn't *all* you should feed your children for breakfast—just what you should be feeding them *most* of the time. Routines are comforting to children (and adults), so your kids will eventually settle into good eating habits if you guide them properly. Consider the fact that my dad has devoured a peanut butter and jelly sandwich for lunch nearly every day for about 70 years! Eating habits formed early can last a lifetime.

BREAKFAST: PAR FOODS

Eat these no more than two or three times a week:
- muffins (apple, blueberry, bran)
- apricots, cantaloupe, papaya, pineapple, raisins
- higher-fiber pancakes or waffles made with whole-grain wheat or buckwheat; add fresh berries to make them really delicious; experiment with adding ground flaxseed to pancake/waffle mix for fiber and nutrients
- whole-grain or pumpernickel bagels with low-fat cream cheese;
- grits; add Smart Balance–type spread and enjoy, especially as a more wholesome replacement for fried potatoes alongside eggs
- eggs, seven per week maximum (eggs are a rich source of choline, an important brain nutrient)
- cheese, featuring low GL and high calcium
- sweetened yogurt (most store brands)
- lean-cut bacon or Canadian bacon, no more than once or twice a week

Actually, I'd give that bacon a "Par/Bogey" rating. Incidentally, my wife's 95-year-old grandmother ate a piece of bacon, an egg, and half a grapefruit every morning for most of her life. Her secret: not overeating or snacking between meals.

As for pancakes and waffles, use low-sugar syrup—and resist using a large amount. Buckwheat, meanwhile, is not wheat at all—and is a nutritious, high-fiber choice for those on a gluten-free diet.

BREAKFAST: BOGEY FOODS

Avoid these as much as possible, having them once a week at most:
- doughnuts, cinnamon rolls, scones, regular and "instant" pastries (Pop Tarts, toaster strudel, etc.)
- plain bagels, which are calorie-dense with high glycemic loads
- cereals, breads, and biscuits that have high GI and/or GL
- refined sugar
- dates, "fruit" roll-ups
- sausage
- hash browns and other fried potatoes

LUNCH: BIRDIE FOODS

Serve plenty of these:
- whole-grain breads for sandwiches (it's whole-grain if that's the first item on the "ingredients" list, and the dietary fiber content is three grams or more)
- peanut butter (natural is best, with no or low added sugar)
- hummus spread for sandwiches or dip
- avocados, tomatoes, and peppers; avocados are rich in antioxidants and "good" monounsaturated fat, but are very calorie-dense, so eat them in small quantities
- soups (homemade are best), especially tomato, lentil, and minestrone

- fresh vegetables including broccoli, carrots, mushrooms, zucchini, cauliflower, and eggplant; letting your child dip them in a little light ranch dressing is okay
- all kinds of legumes (beans), including three-bean salad
- extra virgin olive oil or no-trans-fat butter spread on whole-grain bread; among oils, olive, canola, flaxseed, and peanut are highest in omega-3 and monounsaturated fat
- pastas and noodles made with whole grain and cooked to maintain firmness
- nuts and seeds: almonds, walnuts, sunflower seeds, peanuts (technically a legume), etc.; don't offer more than two tablespoons at a time
- tofu, an excellent protein source that can be added to soups and sandwiches
- low-fat cottage cheese
- two percent (age one and over) or skim (age two and over) milk, water, decaffeinated tea
- "Birdie" foods from the breakfast and dinner lists

LUNCH: PAR FOODS

The following should be limited to two or three times a week:
- lean chicken, turkey, or beef sliced for sandwiches
- tuna ("chunk light" in water is best) or egg salad for sandwiches; use a mayonnaise substitute made from canola oil
- soups, especially black bean, green pea, split pea, canned minestrone, tomato, and chicken noodle
- blue corn tortilla chips with sugar-free salsa and/or guacamole
- macaroni and cheese made with whole-grain macaroni

- cheese
- pasta salad (see recipe in Chapter 17)
- light or air-popped popcorn (remove unpopped seeds to avoid aspiration)
- "Par" foods from the breakfast and dinner lists

LUNCH: BOGEY FOODS

While you may not have to ban these, it's best to avoid them:
- processed lunchmeats (I enjoy Italian subs, but try to limit them to once every couple of weeks)
- non-whole-grain bread and crackers; rice cakes, pretzels; graham crackers (all nutritionally unnecessary and high-GI)
- French fries, especially from fast food restaurants (one of the worst things you can feed your children)
- burgers, pizza, hot dogs, etc.
- "Bogey" foods from the breakfast and dinner lists

Does cutting out "Bogey" foods really make a dent in obesity? Consider Steve, a high school student I've seen for years. At age 14, Steve was 66 inches tall and weighed 157 pounds, for a BMI of 25.3; he was very near the 95th percentile.

We talked about diet and exercise; he determined to eat a bit better. By cutting out the "greasy pizza and fries" at lunch, and not "eating ice cream every night before bedtime," he was able to thin down without doing anything else.

He recently saw me for an exam; he was still losing weight and happy with that, though his mom wanted to be sure nothing was amiss. He weighed 146 pounds and was 70 inches tall, for a BMI of 20.9—the 50th percentile for his age! He checked out fine, with no signs of illness.

DINNER: BIRDIE FOODS

Here are the suppertime staples to major in:
- vegetables, fruits, legumes
- whole-grain breads, dinner rolls, and biscuits; pour extra virgin olive oil onto a plate as a condiment
- whole-grain tortillas
- salads made with lots of vegetables, a variety of lettuce types, and olive- or canola-oil-based dressings
- brown and long-grain unprocessed rice, and other whole grains
- whole-grain pastas with marinara or pesto sauce
- "Birdie" foods from the breakfast and lunch lists
- fish that are high in omega-3 fatty acids

And now, a few words about fish.

The evidence is clear: Fish can be good for your heart. If possible, eat two six-ounce servings a week (two ounces twice a week for smaller children, age two and up, increasing to six ounces for adults).

Now comes the tricky part: Which fish are best? The answer isn't altogether clear, but we want species that are high in omega-3 fatty acids and low in mercury. Ingestion of mercury is especially a concern for women planning pregnancy, those currently pregnant, and children under age 2.

Cold-water fish (flounder, wild salmon, sardines, chunk light tuna, pollock, ahi tuna, yellowtail) are highest in healthful omega-3 fatty acids. Shrimp are fairly high in omega-3 and contain little or no mercury, but are higher in fat and cholesterol. Larger predator fish (swordfish, king mackerel, shark, tilefish) are highest in mercury. Ahi tuna, yellowtail, white chunk "albacore" tuna, tuna steak, and halibut recently have been implicated as moderately high in mercury, but not as high as the predators.

The U.S. Food and Drug Administration (FDA) says that a person who isn't pregnant or under age two can safely eat up to six ounces of the moderately mercury-containing fish weekly. Two servings a week of the lowest-mercury fish are okay.

When you prepare fish, cut away any fat and skin before serving; don't eat any innards, such as the liver. Be sure all bones are removed. My recommendation for kids is to stick with wild salmon and chunk light tuna.

Salmon has the highest level of omega-3—and one of the lowest levels of mercury. Chunk light tuna is second in the omega-3 ratings. I prefer wild salmon to farm-raised, though it may cost more.

For more information on fish, consult your physician—and the FDA and Environmental Protection Agency Web sites (www.cpa.gov and www.fda.gov).

DINNER: PAR FOODS

You can enjoy these foods twice or thrice weekly unless otherwise noted:

- "Par" foods from the breakfast and lunch lists
- lean, non-sausage meats; whenever possible, grill the meat so the fat drips off; always trim off any charred sections; for stew or beef chili, boil meat first if you can, skimming off and discarding the fat
- shrimp (a serving once a week or once every two weeks)
- regular pasta
- potatoes—boiled new, baked russet, sweet, and white
- couscous, sweet corn
- tortillas

Note that meat should not exceed 25 percent of the meal, with the serving no bigger than the palm of the eater's hand or a deck of cards. Offering a salad, vegetables, or whole-grain bread with olive oil before the main course can dampen hunger and make smaller meat portions less noticeable. Eating lean meats several times per week can be a valuable part of a balanced diet, helping to fulfill your child's protein and iron requirements.

DINNER: BOGEY FOODS

Just say no to these as often as you can:
- "Bogey" foods from the breakfast and lunch lists
- pizza (you might have this once every two weeks as a treat, but order it with less meat and more vegetables, and have a salad first)
- fast foods
- fried foods
- instant, red, French fried, and mashed potatoes ("smashed" potatoes are better since the skin is included)
- biscuits and dinner rolls (non-whole-grain)

YOUR KIDS MAY SURPRISE YOU

You may be saying, "But, Dr. Andersen, there's no way my kids will eat the 'healthy' stuff on that list!" Don't panic. And don't be too sure about what your children may develop a taste for.

When my daughter Heather was six, our family took a vacation. One day, in a restaurant, a waitress walked by with a plate of oysters on the half shell. Not being a fan of the slimy little creatures, I didn't give them a second look. But Heather did.

"Dad, what are those things?" she asked.

"Oysters."

"Oysters. Are they good?"

"They're okay, but I don't care for them. Do you want to try some?" I thought I was safe with that question; no way would she want to try something as exotic as an oyster.

"Sure!" came her swift and enthusiastic reply.

To my astonishment, she ate not one but several. Lesson: You never know what kids may try or learn to like. Sometimes you just have to give them a chance.

CHAPTER SEVENTEEN

MENUS AND RECIPES

N eed help picturing what your child's meals should look like? This chapter includes a sample one-week menu and a selection of recipes.

WHAT'S FOR DINNER–AND OTHER MEALS, TOO

These sample menus allow for a nice variety of dishes. You'll probably want to add more dinner entrée choices.

Having a healthful, substantial breakfast each day should be the rock on which wholesome eating rests. Teens are especially prone to skipping this meal, but that can lead to paradoxical weight gain.

Some of the meals described have quite a few offerings for variety; you don't have to serve everything listed. Just remember to eat slowly with smaller portions.

I haven't included dessert suggestions. If you want to enjoy a few, remember: moderation.

Day 1

Breakfast: Equal parts of Post Original Shredded Wheat 'N Bran Spoon Size mixed with raisin bran or Cheerios, plus milk; add blueberries, raspberries, blackberries, or strawberries. For children age seven and older, add a few almonds or walnuts. A small glass of grapefruit juice and a banana or some grapes can be included, too.

Lunch: Sandwich with whole-grain bread and turkey; add a slice of cheese, lettuce, and tomato per taste; Dijon mustard or canola mayonnaise are nice spreads to use. You could add whole-grain crackers or a palm-sized serving of nuts (vary by type daily); an apple (or green pepper slices or other fresh vegetables); and milk and water. Occasionally include a small piece of dark chocolate as a treat.

Dinner: Salad with mixed greens and olive oil–based dressing; experiment with adding petite vegetables, green peppers, black olives, and cherry tomatoes. Include whole-grain bread with olive oil or Smart Balance spread; vegetable (offer a different one with different color at each meal); Tuna Noodle Casserole (see recipe; no additional vegetable needed); milk and water.

Day 2

Breakfast: Non-instant oatmeal with raisins and/or berries added if desired (add Splenda to sweeten if you prefer); whole-grain toast with peanut or almond butter or Smart Balance spread; half grapefruit; milk and water.

Lunch: Lentil soup (see recipe) and sandwich with thin-sliced lean beef or grilled cheese (use whole-grain bread and low-fat cheese); apple or grapes (cut into small pieces for younger children); milk and water.

Dinner: Fresh broccoli and green peppers with light ranch dressing; whole-grain bread with olive oil and Parmesan cheese; black beans or baked beans; chicken breast dish (see recipes), grilled or pan-fried in canola oil. Remember, only a palm-sized piece—the palm size of the person consuming. Don't forget milk and water.

Day 3

Breakfast: High-fiber cereal with milk; eggs and whole-grain toast if still hungry; fresh fruit (orange slices, for instance); milk and/or fresh juice.

Lunch: Sandwich (peanut butter and low-sugar jam or jelly); yogurt; nuts; apple (an apple a day really is a great way to eat well); milk and water.

Dinner: Vegetable or tomato soup; salad; Mexican wraps with tofu, avocado, sprouts, salsa (use whole-grain tortillas); fresh fruit if still hungry; milk and water.

Day 4

Breakfast: High-fiber cereal with milk and banana or other fruit; whole-grain muffin or bagel with light cream cheese; grapefruit juice.

Lunch: Tuna salad sandwich; low-fat cottage cheese; grapes or apple or berries; milk and water.

Dinner: Salad with walnuts, pear slices, and raspberry vinaigrette dressing; whole-grain bread with spread or olive oil; whole-grain rice or sweet potato; green beans; grilled salmon; milk and water.

Day 5

Breakfast: High-fiber cereal with milk; fruit; whole-grain toast; milk and/or grapefruit juice.

Lunch: Egg salad sandwich; nuts; apple or other fruit (like peaches, grapes, oranges, plums, cherries); milk or water.

Dinner: Salad; corn on the cob (in season) or other vegetable; chicken (grilled in summer) or turkey dish; whole-grain bread or rolls; milk and water.

Day 6

Breakfast: Eggs, grits, and whole-grain toast; milk and/or grape-fruit juice.

Lunch: Soup and/or sandwich with turkey or lean pastrami (cut off excess fat); whole-grain crackers and/or nuts; apple or other fruit; milk or water.

Dinner: Blue corn tortilla chips and salsa; fresh vegetables with light ranch dip or salsa; chili (see recipe); milk and water.

Day 7

Breakfast: Whole-grain pancakes (see recipe) with Smart Balance spread and light syrup, adding berries if desired; lean bacon or Canadian bacon; milk and juice.

Lunch: Soup and/or sandwich or pasta salad; yogurt; fruit; milk and water.

Dinner: Lettuce salad or fresh fruit salad; vegetable; Zesty Roast Beef (see recipe) or grilled beef dish in summer; whole-grain bread; milk and water.

This is just a sample meal schedule; mix and match as you see fit, and add your own recipes. Remember that many items—pancake mix, pasta salad, egg salad, tuna salad, chili, stew, lentil soup—can be made in advance, kept in the refrigerator, and eaten for several days. Chili, stew, marinara sauce, and soups can be made in bulk and frozen—a real timesaver for busy working parents.

THE RECIPE BOX

I'm not a good cook; I owe it to my wife that I'm not underfed. Here are a few dishes she's perfected and that we've enjoyed for years.

There's nothing fancy here—just regular fare that most families will find appealing. But it's much more wholesome than the food some families are currently consuming. This will give you a place to start as you improve your eating habits. (Note: Serving estimates are based on adult portions.) *Bon appétit!*

Breakfast

Whole Wheat Pancakes

2 cups Hodgson Mill Insta-Bake Whole Wheat Variety Baking Mix with Buttermilk

2 eggs

1¹/4 cups skim milk

2 tablespoons canola oil

No need to use sugar; these are very good without it. If you like, add a little Splenda to sweeten. Combine ingredients in a bowl and mix until smooth. Pour desired amount of batter onto a hot griddle sprayed with canola oil. Makes about 10 five-inch pancakes.

Lunch or Dinner

Lentil Soup

1-pound bag of lentils

8 cups of water

¹/2 to ³/4 cup chopped carrots

2 tablespoons chopped onions

¹/2 teaspoon salt

¹/2 teaspoon dried oregano

¹/4 teaspoon ground black pepper

Optional: 1 cup diced lean ham

Wash and drain lentils (no need to soak them). Place them in a large pot with 8 cups of warm water. Add the other ingredients, cover, and bring to a boil. Then lower heat and simmer for 45 minutes to an hour. Stir frequently. Lentil soup is naturally quite thick; you can add

water, chicken broth, or beef broth to thin as desired. Lentils are very
high in fiber. Serves about 8.

Pasta Salad
12-ounce package of whole wheat pasta
    (bow tie, elbow, or rigatoni)
4 tablespoons olive oil
About 30 black olives, halved
1 cup of zucchini in small cubes
About 30 cherry or grape tomatoes, halved
$1/2$ cup chopped green pepper (or $1/2$ cup of chopped raw broccoli)
1 cup of cubed cheddar or Monterey Jack cheese
3-4 tablespoons of fresh oregano, finely chopped
    Boil pasta according to package directions; don't overcook. Drain
and transfer to a bowl; while it's still hot, sprinkle with olive oil and
mix thoroughly. Let cool slightly, then add remaining ingredients and
stir. Sprinkle lightly with salt and pepper to taste. Refrigerate for at
least one hour before serving. Makes about 10 cups; I'd serve about $1/2$
cup to smaller kids and 1 cup to older children.

Dinner
Apricot Chicken
1 teaspoon dried thyme
$1/2$ teaspoon salt
$2/3$ cup apricot preserves
4 tablespoons balsamic vinegar
Ground pepper
3 or 4 boneless, skinless chicken breast halves (if larger, about $1/2$
    chicken breast per person; otherwise $3/4$-1 each)
    Sprinkle both sides of chicken breasts with dried thyme and salt.
Spray canola or olive oil cooking spray onto a non-stick skillet at

medium heat. Cook chicken until done, about 7-8 minutes per side. Remove chicken from heat as soon as it's no longer pink inside. While the chicken cooks, combine apricot preserves, balsamic vinegar, and a dash of pepper in a bowl. Set cooked chicken aside and cover to keep warm. Pour the apricot preserve/balsamic vinegar mix into the skillet; simmer on medium heat until bubbly, stirring constantly. Drizzle over chicken and serve immediately. Serves 3-4.

Chicken Cacciatore
3 tablespoons chopped onion
1 small clove of garlic, finely chopped
2 teaspoons dried rosemary or oregano
$1/2$ cup chicken broth
15-ounce can of drained, diced tomatoes
$1/2$ teaspoon salt
$1/4$-$1/2$ teaspoon crushed red pepper flakes
4 boneless, skinless chicken breast halves
Olive oil cooking spray

Spray a non-stick skillet with olive oil cooking spray; cook chicken over medium heat until done, turning frequently. Remove, place on a plate, and cover to keep warm. Add onion, garlic, and rosemary to the skillet and cook for 2 minutes. Add chicken broth and heat for another 2 minutes. Add tomatoes, cover, and simmer on low heat for about 10 minutes. Add chicken back to the skillet and warm for a few minutes. Serves 6-8.

Chicken Fajitas
Whole wheat soft tortillas
4 skinless chicken breast halves
2 large chopped tomatoes
1 green pepper, sliced into strips

1 onion, sliced into strips

3 avocados

1 small jar salsa

1 small package shredded Monterey Jack cheese (use about 4 oz)

Ground black pepper

Chili pepper

Paprika

Olive oil cooking spray

Grill chicken or cook on stove top as in previous recipes. Cut into small pieces, sprinkle lightly with salt, paprika, pepper, and chili powder; stir and set aside. Sauté green pepper and onions for about 2 minutes in olive oil–coated skillet. Mash avocados until smoothly textured and add salsa to make guacamole. The amount you add depends on how spicy you'd like it to be. Place tomatoes, guacamole, shredded cheese, chicken, and extra salsa in separate bowls. Warm tortillas. You may want to serve buffet style. Makes about 8 fajitas.

Tuna and Noodle Casserole

12-ounce package of whole wheat wide, curly noodles

1 10.75-ounce can of fat-free cream of mushroom soup

10 ounces skim milk

2 six-ounce cans of chunk light tuna in water, drained

1 tablespoon fresh tarragon, finely chopped

1 cup frozen peas

Boil noodles according to package directions; drain and place in a casserole dish. Combine other ingredients in a bowl, pour over noodles, and mix thoroughly. Sprinkle lightly with pepper. Bake uncovered at 350 degrees for about 20 minutes—until it starts to bubble and is slightly crisp on top. (I like to splash a bit of Tabasco sauce over mine to spice it up; my wife thinks I'm crazy.) Serves 5-6.

Three Bean Chili

2 15-ounce cans of tomato sauce with Italian herbs

2 14½-ounce cans of diced tomatoes

1 15-ounce can of dark kidney beans

1 15-ounce can of red beans

1 15-ounce can of chili beans

1 medium green pepper, diced

1 medium red pepper, diced

1 small zucchini, diced

2 tablespoons chopped onions

1 level teaspoon Hershey's cocoa powder

½ teaspoon salt

¼ teaspoon ground black pepper (adjust to taste)

1 teaspoon Tabasco sauce (adjust to taste)

1 teaspoon chili powder (adjust to taste)

If you like it hotter, add one small hot pepper, finely chopped

Optional: 2 boneless, skinless chicken breast halves or one
    turkey breast

The vegetarian version is wonderful, low-fat and high-fiber. Combine all the ingredients in a large pot and simmer for an hour or so, stirring frequently. If desired, add chicken or turkey; cut the meat into bite-sized pieces. Coat a skillet with cooking oil spray and cook chicken over medium heat until done (about 10 minutes), stirring regularly. When chicken is done, drain and add to other ingredients. Simmer for about 30 minutes after adding chicken. Serves 6-8.

Beef, Lamb, or Venison Stew

2½ cups water

1 cup beef broth

2 .87-ounce packages of onion gravy mix

1 tablespoon packed brown sugar

2 teaspoons ground thyme

Dash of black pepper to taste

1 pound of lean, trimmed beef, lamb, or venison cut into
    bite-sized pieces

6 carrots cut into 1-inch pieces

2 turnips cut into 1-inch cubes (far fewer calories than potatoes)

1 cup frozen peas

Olive oil cooking spray

Boil meat in water (about 5 minutes for smaller pieces, 6-7 minutes for larger chunks). Drain and set meat aside. Or cook meat in a skillet with olive oil (be careful not to overcook), draining off the fat. In a large pot, combine water plus all the ingredients except the meat and peas; simmer over medium heat. Add the meat, simmering for 1-1½ hours, stirring occasionally. Add extra beef broth or water to adjust thickness as desired. Add peas and cook for 10 minutes more. Serves 4-6.

Zesty Roast Beef

2½ pounds boneless beef eye of round (less fat than other beef
    roasts)

2 14½-ounce cans diced tomatoes

1 cup V8 tomato juice

2 bay leaves

2 teaspoons beef bouillon granules or 2 crushed cubes

4 tablespoons chopped onion

2 teaspoons dried basil

3 tablespoons fresh chopped parsley

¼ teaspoon pepper

5 medium turnips cut into cubes

8 carrots, sliced into 1-inch pieces (peeling optional)

Olive oil cooking spray

Trim fat from meat. Spray a Dutch oven with olive oil spray; coat the meat lightly with flour and brown briefly on all sides over medium heat. Add diced tomatoes, V8 juice, bay leaves, beef bouillon, onion, basil, parsley, and pepper. Bring to a boil; cover and simmer for two hours. During the last 45 minutes, add carrots and turnips. When meat is cooked, remove it to a carving plate and let cool for 5 minutes before slicing into thin pieces, cutting against the grain of the meat. Serve along with the carrots and turnips, pouring the gravy from the pan over the other ingredients. If gravy is too thin, combine 1 table-spoon of cornstarch with 2 tablespoons cool water in a cup; stir well, add to gravy, and simmer to desired thickness. Serves about 6.

Salmon Fillets

1 pound salmon fillets

2 tablespoons fresh cilantro, chopped (or substitute fresh, chopped tarragon or dill)

1 lemon, cut into slim wedges

Olive oil cooking spray

Preheat oven to 350 degrees. Place salmon, skin side down, into an olive oil–coated baking dish. Squeeze a little lemon juice onto the fish. Sprinkle cilantro over the top and bake uncovered for approximately 8-10 minutes. Salmon is done when it flakes easily with a fork. Serve on a warm plate surrounded with cilantro and the remaining lemon wedges. This dish is wonderful with warm, crusty wheat bread, asparagus, and a bowl of fresh berries. Serves 3-4.

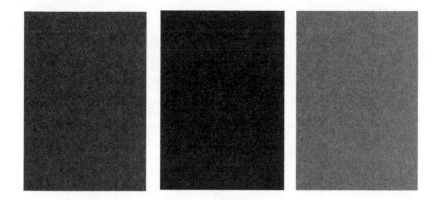

PART SEVEN

MAINTAINING
MOMENTUM

CHAPTER EIGHTEEN

KEEPING IT FUN AND KEEPING IT GOING

Ask anyone who's "dieted," and you'll likely hear that it wasn't an enjoyable or rewarding experience. A glance in the mirror after losing some weight might have sparked some smiles, but not the actual process. Diet regimens often involve conscious hunger, and can isolate one from family and peers.

That's why it's crucial to have the whole family involved in the life-changing recommendations I've been talking about. Done properly, it shouldn't be an unpleasant chore but a step in the right direction. Your child shouldn't be complaining of hunger; on the contrary, he may be more satisfied and have fewer cravings.

Some bad snacking habits will take time to break. But break they will if you demonstrate resolve—not in a punitive way, but in a quiet commitment to doing things differently as a family. It's very important that your child views these changes not as punishment, but just as the way things are going to be from now on.

You may want to frame these adjustments as ones you need to make for yourself. And because they're healthy changes, the kids are included.

GETTING YOUR FAMILY ON BOARD

So that your child doesn't feel confused or isolated, your entire family needs to board the fitness express. Kids can handle huge changes readily if their parents and siblings are alongside. With creativity, you can make physical activities and dietary makeovers fun and rewarding for all involved—and, to be successful, you must.

I have the pleasure of seeing children of all races, creeds, and backgrounds. I can tell you that no family is immune from the potential problem of obesity. But diverse experiences, as well as cultural and religious beliefs, can substantially influence a family's attitude toward dealing with it.

One such family I saw was made up of two professional parents and three children. Two of the kids were considerably overweight, as was the mom. This was a number of years ago, before the obesity epidemic was front and center; the mom simply had been unaware of the perils of excess weight.

As I delicately opened discussion of these children's obesity, the mom made it clear to me that she wasn't concerned with the kids' appearances; the family's Christian faith focused on the soul. The mom seemed relieved to know that I shared her beliefs concerning the soul. As I proceeded to reason with her about the dangers of obesity, we agreed that our faith did not preclude care of the physical body, but in fact encouraged it.

In the Bible, our bodies are called the temple of the Holy Spirit. They're to be used to serve God and others, so caring for them is important. "Or do you not know that your body is the temple of the Holy Spirit who is in you, whom you have from God, and you are not your own? For you were bought at a price; therefore glorify God in your body and in your spirit, which are God's" (1 Corinthians 6:19-20).

For Christian families, motivating by grace is the most powerful way. In other words, "Look what God has done for us. We belong to Him, so we should care for ourselves out of gratitude to Him." This truth can be presented to children, helping them understand why it's important to make changes geared toward better health.

This, by the way, is not self-worship; it's respecting God's ownership of our bodies. If you borrowed your parents' car, would you beat it up and neglect it? I hope not. So why beat up and neglect the "vehicle" God has given you?

Most children—especially young ones—are driven by a natural desire to please their parents. And fear of punishment (the "stick") and hope of reward (the "carrot") hold an important place in childrearing. But unconditional love and acceptance are difficult to beat when it comes to gaining a child's respect, affection, and cooperation.

THE REWARDS OF REWARDS

Appeals to faith and relationship don't negate the value of more tangible encouragement. You can motivate younger children with simple rewards such as star stickers on a chart, extra reading before bedtime, or trips to the zoo. Most important are hugs, kisses, and loving, sincere praise.

Older children, despite their frequent protestations to the contrary, thrive on the love and support of parents and siblings. Nudge them along with rewards like a favorite CD, a trip to a movie, or a sleepover with friends (quietly arrange for light popcorn and diet soft drinks to be the only snacks available). Offer these occasionally and spontaneously for consistency of effort, rather than using them as a bribe.

One powerful motivation for your child to participate in a fitness program is to see *you* doing it. Spending time with others who are interested in fitness can also be a tremendous motivator.

As your child grows, consider joining a sports and fitness center where he can be around people who are fit and active. Most centers are packed with fun activities for children; some have special hours when kids can swim, run, and play ball. It's not only great fun, but creates a positive image of physical exercise.

When on vacation, plan activities that continue the progress you're making. Hike, swim, play tennis, go for long walks.

I remember traveling to Florida as a child each summer. It was hot, but we didn't care. We'd spend all day swimming, walking up and down the beach, and playing tennis. Rarely did we watch TV. Come bedtime, my sister and I would crash. We were out cold in minutes, which no doubt came as a relief to our folks.

The point is that we got to do what kids will do if given the chance: run around and play. For kids, freedom is its own reward.

This doesn't mean you should spend your vacations obsessing about fitness. If you've been maintaining a healthy routine at home, your body will be better able to handle a short "splurge" of treats or sedentary behavior. That can make vacationing more enjoyable as you concentrate on relaxing with your family instead of on how much weight you might gain.

BACKSLIDING, HOPE, AND LOVE

Kids who've lost weight will often gain some back—or rebel against your guidance. One girl, Annie, was successful at first. But she lost momentum and regained some pounds. She knew why: She'd begun to eat poorly again due to laziness and social pressure.

What should you do if your child backslides or rebels?

There's no foolproof response to this. But parental consistency is vital. Once your family has tasted success, you know it's possible. This is half the battle; it keeps hope alive and squelches defeatism. Simply staying the course and continuing to model proper health behavior is my best advice.

Rebellion is much tougher to handle. But I know what *doesn't* work—trying to coerce recalcitrant kids into toeing the line.

Your best—and most biblical—response is to love your child unconditionally, pray for her, and set reasonable boundaries. Your genuine, demonstrated love is likely to elicit a grateful response.

So remember: Hang in there! Try to keep it light, despite the seriousness of the matter. Help your child to enjoy his or her newfound freedom from old, bad habits. That's the way to keep it going.

CHAPTER NINETEEN

ACTIVITIES AND FITNESS RESOURCES

Want to prevent or overcome childhood obesity? There's nothing like daily exercise to help you do just that. The physical and psychological benefits of getting and staying active will speed your child down the path to fitness.

In this chapter you'll find activities and routines you can use with children of any age—and guidelines on how to perform them properly. Tweak these patterns to fit your family.

If you're not sure what your child can do, ask your doctor. If you want a more structured or detailed program, seek the help of a personal trainer. Available at most health clubs, a personal trainer can tailor an exercise regimen to your child.

In any case, start doing something! If the activities in this chapter seem too daunting, begin by taking a walk with your child each evening. Work your way up to working out.

LET'S GET MOVING!

The following activities are appropriate for girls and boys; both can benefit from increased muscle mass and strength, thus increasing their Basal Metabolic Rate (BMR).

Warm up, exercise, then stretch. Ramp up slowly; once you find a good starting point for your child, don't increase the difficulty of the exercises more often than every two weeks.

At first, some children may have difficulty doing these exercises. Encourage them to give it a try and not to give up.

How do you do that, especially if they resist getting started?

Participate with them. Gently support them. Emphasize that they're not competing with anyone, and can proceed at their own pace. If they can complete only one "knee" push-up, great! It's a start. Two will be your next goal.

Emphasize present benefits; tell them they'll be faster, stronger, less tired, and better at soccer, baseball, or cheerleading. Children have trouble connecting the present with the future, so lecturing them about reductions in heart disease and diabetes isn't likely to move them.

Keep track of progress. You can monitor only what you can measure, so you need objective yardsticks of success. Exercise lends itself well to this; you can count the number of minutes walked, push-ups done, or curls performed. Draw up a chart with the days of the week on top and activities on the left, and keep it up to date.

It's easy to feel overwhelmed by the prospect of starting an exercise program. But as I discovered after having hip replacement surgery a few years ago, a big journey is completed in small steps. Simply putting weight on my leg was difficult at first. I wondered if I'd ever be normal again.

But then I was able to take several steps with the aid of crutches.

Several turned into 10, then 20. Soon the crutches were no longer necessary, and I used a cane. I never knew it could be so thrilling just to walk without a cane.

A seemingly impossible task is always intimidating. The pyramids took shape one stone at a time. Rome wasn't built in a day. The Chicago Cubs . . . never mind, I won't go there. Just be sure to provide positive strokes for your child—and assure him that everyone has room for improvement.

Here are the exercises and stretches. I'll teach them to you, and you can teach your child.

Push-ups

This is a tremendous activity for building and toning the triceps and chest muscles as well as the muscles of the abdomen/core.

Depending on your fitness level, this exercise can be performed on your toes or your knees (the latter is easier). Face the floor with a straight spine. Your palms should be a bit to the side and in front of your shoulders. Hold your head in line with your spine; contract your abdominal muscles while you slowly lower your body until your chest is near the floor. In a smooth and controlled motion, push back up to your starting position. Your elbows should be slightly bent but not fully extended. Immediately repeat the process, with no pauses.

Inhale when lowering your body; exhale when pushing up. Do two sets of eight to twelve repetitions, or as many as you can handle with good technique. If you can't complete a set on your toes, finish on your knees.

As you grow stronger, slow the repetitions or place your feet on the edge of a couch for a bit more challenge. Keep your body rigid as a plank with no bend at the waist, tightening your abdominal muscles. For even more challenge, try fingertip push-ups.

Sit-ups (Crunches)

These strengthen and tone your abdominal muscles (the "abs").

Lie on your back with your knees bent. Your feet should be flat on the floor, hip-width apart, hands at your side. Tighten your abs, keeping your spine in a neutral position; think about pushing the small of your back toward the floor. Lift your shoulders slowly off the ground (avoid straining your neck forward); then, while maintaining contraction of the abs, slowly lower back down. Try not to lower your shoulders all the way to the floor so as to maintain constant tightening of the abs.

Do two to three sets of twelve to fifteen repetitions. Don't perform the sets sequentially, but do other exercises in between. To increase the difficulty, perform the exercise while holding your legs off the ground with the knees and hips bent at ninety degrees.

To work the sides of your abdominal muscles, try "bicycle" crunches. With your feet elevated, do a constant crunch while alternately touching the left elbow to the right knee and the right elbow to the left knee. Continue for thirty to sixty seconds.

Pull-ups and Chin-ups

These can be done on a chin-up bar at home or the monkey bars at the park. They're an excellent way to tone and strengthen muscles of the upper back, biceps, and forearms. With pull-ups (more difficult), palms face away from you as you grip the bar. With chin-ups, palms face you.

Position hands slightly wider than your shoulders. Slowly pull the weight of your body up until your chin is level with the bar. Lower yourself in a smooth, controlled fashion; repeat. If this proves too difficult, make the exercise easier by having someone gently lift you at the waist. If possible, stabilize your legs to prevent your body from swinging.

This is a tough exercise, but one that can build strength quickly. Remember to breathe properly, inhaling while lowering and exhaling while pulling up. Do as many repetitions as possible, increasing to a maximum of twelve. If you can do two sets of eight to twelve each, you'll be very fit indeed.

Back-ups ("Supermans")

These tone the lower back and muscles of the buttocks.

Lie on your stomach while lifting your arms and legs off the ground and holding them up like Superman in flight. You can also have your arms at your side, palms facing upward. Point your face toward the floor at all times to avoid neck strain. Stay in that position for thirty to sixty seconds, remembering not to hold your breath. Do this two or three times.

Military Press

This targets your shoulders, upper back, and triceps.

Using two dumbbells, starting in the two- to five-pound range, sit in a chair with good back support. Rest the weights on your thighs. Lift the weights to shoulder level; slowly press them toward the ceiling, then slowly lower them. Keep your elbows relaxed at the top; don't lock them.

Repeat without breaking rhythm, maintaining a smooth, unhurried pace. Start with two sets of eight to twelve repetitions.

Biceps Curls

Start with two-pound dumbbells. Stand with your feet shoulder-width apart, holding the weights at your side. Stand tall with shoulders back and down. As you draw in your abdominal muscles, curl the weight upward so that your palm faces and approaches the shoulder.

Smoothly lower and repeat. Perform two sets of eight to twelve repetitions.

Triceps Extensions

This exercise works the triceps muscle group on the back of the upper arm, one of the most important in sports. Holding a two- to five-pound weight, extend your arms up and behind you, holding the weight just above and behind the shoulder. Slowly push the weight up, using the triceps muscles instead of the shoulder muscles, completing eight to twelve repetitions. Complete two sets, alternating with biceps curls.

Triceps Dips

You won't need weights for this one. Sit on the edge of a chair or bench. Grab the edge with both hands, palms facing the floor, fingers wrapped around the edge at the sides of your legs.

Now lift your buttocks and "walk" away from the chair, keeping hold of it until your buttocks is fully off the chair. You'll bend slightly at the waist. Slowly lower your buttocks toward the floor, using your triceps muscles; then push back up. Maintain a constant angle between your torso and your legs, and don't lock your elbows. Try to keep your elbows as close to your sides as possible. Two sets of eight to twelve will have those triceps burning!

Lunges

This is one of the most effective lower body exercises, good for strengthening thighs and buttocks. Don't use weights at the start. Later, to add difficulty, perform the exercise while holding light dumbbells at your sides.

Standing tall with arms hanging at your side, take a large step forward. As your foot touches the floor, bend both knees until the lead thigh is parallel to the floor and the other thigh is perpendicular to it. The rear foot stays put. Once the knee on that side approaches the ground, press up off the ball of your foot with the front leg and step back to the starting position.

Now repeat with the opposite leg stepping forward. Continue until each leg has done eight to twelve repetitions. Complete two sets.

Squats

These are fabulous for the muscles of the thigh and buttocks.

Stand tall, feet about shoulder-width apart or slightly wider. Extend your arms straight ahead with palms facing the floor. While keeping your back straight and looking ahead, slowly squat until your thighs are about parallel to the ground. Slowly return to the starting position, concentrating on contracting buttock muscles and thighs. Your knees shouldn't extend forward over your toes.

Perform eight to twelve repetitions. Repeat after doing some other exercises. Holding weights in your hands will add to the difficulty, as will balancing on a Bosu Balance Trainer.

Calf Raises

These strengthen the calf muscles. While balancing against a door or chair with ankles tilted slightly forward, push up on one or both feet until the ankle is fully extended. Lower back down. Work each side, doing two sets of eight to twelve repetitions.

Jumping Rope

A $15 jump rope with ball bearings, available at sporting goods stores, lets you engage in this fantastic cardiovascular and strengthening exercise.

Keep your arms away from your side and as still as possible. By using your wrists and a little arm motion, jump rope for a few minutes to start. Keep the rope low to the ground and stay light on your feet. Slowly increase the time spent on this exercise, which is a tremendous calorie burner and a muscle builder for arms and legs.

WHEN AND HOW TO EXERCISE

The resistance training exercises I've just described can be done at most ages. Push-ups, sit-ups, pull-ups, back-ups, lunges, and calf raises can be done without access to free weights.

For exercises using weights, here's a rule of thumb: When you can comfortably perform two sets of twelve repetitions at a certain weight, move up in two- to five-pound increments. For other exercises, increase repetitions once you can do two sets of twelve.

As workouts get easier, avoid getting sloppy. Proper breathing and technique are important to reaping maximum benefit from any exercise.

Always work opposing muscle groups during the same session. For instance, always do sets of sit-ups and back-ups together—or biceps curls and triceps extensions. These muscle groups balance one another.

You may wish to do lower-body exercises on Monday, Wednesday, and Friday—and upper-body ones on Tuesday, Thursday, and Saturday. You can, however, do all the exercises at one time three to four days a week. Studies have shown that strength training more than four times a week adds no benefit—and may cause harm by leading to excessive muscle fatigue.

If you take more than a week or two off, make sure you ease back into things when you resume. A friend who took an extended vacation wanted to get back to working out when he returned. I reminded him to take it easy, but he wasn't listening. After going all-out his first day back, he felt pretty good that night. But next morning he rediscovered forgotten muscles and walked as if he'd been on a four-day cattle drive!

SMART STRETCHING

Always stretch *after* exercising to maintain maximum suppleness and prevent injury. Don't stretch when muscles are cold. Stretching before exercising isn't necessary, but it's very important to *warm up* before any resistance or aerobic activity.

If you do stretch before you work out, make sure you first walk, jog slowly, or perform any low-impact activity to warm up the muscles. Stretches should be performed slowly, without bouncing. Hold the position for approximately 30 seconds and relax.

Start with the lower body and work up. Here are some stretches, beginning with those you can perform lying down and proceeding to those done in a standing position.

Hamstring Stretch

Sit on the ground, extending your legs at about a 60- to 90-degree angle from each other. Take a deep breath. While you exhale, slowly reach with both hands for the toes of one foot. Keep your leg flat against the ground, but your knee should be "soft." Your face should approach your kneecap as you reach for your toes. Hold for 30 seconds; then repeat with the other leg.

This is an important stretch for people suffering from lower back pain. If your hamstrings are tight, you'll unduly tax your lower back muscles.

Adductor (Groin) Stretch

While sitting, bring your feet together so that the bottom of each foot faces the other. Your knee bend should be a little more than 90 degrees, so that you can comfortably hold on to your feet. Allow your knees to fall to the side while you anchor your feet together. The groin muscles can be further stretched by a slight forward lean. Remember, don't bounce; hold gently for 30 seconds.

Quadriceps (Thigh Muscle) Stretch

Lie on your left side, holding your right foot with your right hand. Gently bring the heel of your right foot toward the right buttocks. You should feel a gentle stretch of the quadriceps muscle in the right leg.

Roll over to the right side and repeat with the left leg. This also can be done in a standing position, holding on to something for balance.

Lower Back Stretch

Lie on your back, knees bent, so that your feet are flat on the floor. Bring one leg up toward your chest, holding it at the knee. As you exhale, gently bring your leg toward your chest. Hold for 30 seconds.

Repeat with the other leg; then do the same with both legs at the same time. You should feel a nice stretch in the lower back muscles.

Abdominal Muscle Stretch and Back Extension ("Cobra" Stretch)

Lie on your stomach. While keeping your pelvis flat on the floor, push up with your arms, to your elbows first. If you're comfortable, raise your chest as high off the ground as possible, resting your palms flat on the floor. Hold for several seconds and lower back down, repeating the process several times.

You should feel a nice stretch of the abdominal muscles; you also may feel a slight crack in the bones of the lower and middle back (which is okay). Follow up by kneeling, resting your buttocks on your heels. Lean forward, bringing your head as close to your knees as possible, stretching the lower back muscles.

Lower Back Rotational Stretch

While lying on your back, take your left leg and move it to the right of your right leg. The right leg will stay straight, while the left will bend at the knee slightly. The thighs should form about a 90-degree angle with the left crossed over the right.

Keep your upper back as flat as possible on the floor with arms extended. The lower back will rotate slowly to the right. Move slowly, and hold for 30 seconds. Repeat with the right leg over the left.

Gastrocnemius (Calf Muscle) Stretch

While standing a few feet from a wall, step toward the wall with one foot while keeping the other foot back. With the back foot flat on the ground, lean forward more and more until you feel a stretch in the calf muscle. Hold for 30 seconds and switch legs.

You can also stand on the edge of a bottom stair step with the front one-third of each foot supported. Slowly allow the weight of the body to stretch the calf muscle.

Upper Back Stretch

Find something sturdy to grab just above waist level (a doorjamb, for instance; you can act as the anchor for your child). Stand facing the object and grab it with both hands. Bend slightly at the knees, arms extended; lean backward, arching the upper back and relaxing the upper back muscles. You should feel a pleasant stretch of those muscles.

This also can be accomplished on your hands and knees. Arch the back upward like a cat, then go in the opposite direction to a "swayback" position. This aids in spine mobility and strength. These back-stretching and strengthening exercises can help a child with back pain due to poor posture, but he or she also needs to work on correcting the cause.

Chest Stretch

While standing in a doorway, place your left elbow, forearm, and hand against the jamb with the upper arm parallel to the floor. Rotate slowly to the right, stretching the left chest muscles. Turn around and do the same with the right arm against the other side of the jamb.

Arm Circles

Stand with arms extended straight out to the side; rotate them slowly in small, concentric circles. Change directions from clockwise to counterclockwise every 30 seconds. Start with small circles. By making the circles slowly larger, you can strengthen and stretch the muscles and ligaments of the shoulders.

Triceps Stretch

Give yourself a pat on the back on the same side as the arm that's doing the patting. While holding that hand on your back, gently push that elbow backward with your other hand, stretching the back of the upper arm. Hold for 30 seconds and move to the other arm.

Posterior Shoulder Stretch

While reaching across your chest with your left arm, keeping the arm parallel to the ground, grab the left elbow with the right hand and bring it gently toward your chest until your left arm is flush to the chest. You should feel a pleasant stretch in the posterior muscles of the shoulder.

Side Stretch

Stand with legs shoulder-width apart, arms extended over your head. Join hands above your head; slowly lean to the left until a stretch is felt in the right side. Hold it for 30 seconds and then switch sides.

These are just a few of the stretches you and your children can do to maintain maximum flexibility. Most kids are very flexible, but overweight children may at first have difficulty—due to their size and a history of decreased range of motion. This makes proper stretching extra important for them.

Your child doesn't have to perform every stretch at every session; but stretch the muscles that have been exercised. These activities may be more fun for younger kids if performed to music or rhymes.

A WEEK'S WORTH OF WORKOUTS

Here's a sample activity program to follow with your child. Modify it to fit your schedule. The eventual goal is 60 minutes of moderate to strenuous activity per day. Don't stare at the "frog" too long; get started!

Monday

Aerobic: Walk thirty minutes, building up gradually; if you can walk for one hour, fantastic. If you'd like to start jogging with your child, go for it. Buy him or her a decent pair of well-fitting shoes and start slowly.

Resistance: Do lower-body exercises along with sit-ups and back-ups; stretch after each session. Note that ankle weights are not recommended for walking or jogging.

Tuesday

Aerobic: Walk, rollerblade, or bicycle for 30 minutes.

Resistance: Do upper-body exercises.

Wednesday

Aerobic: Walk 30 minutes (if you're very busy, take a day off from walking).

Resistance: Do lower-body exercises plus sit-ups and back-ups.

Thursday

Aerobic: Walk, swim, rollerblade, or bicycle for 30 minutes.

Resistance: Do an upper-body workout.

Friday

Aerobic: Walk 30 minutes.

Resistance: Do a lower-body workout with sit-ups and back-ups.

Saturday

Aerobic: Walk, swim, rollerblade, or bicycle for 30 minutes.

Resistance: Do an upper-body workout.

Sunday

Work out if you missed a day. But if you're tired and your child was diligent all week, take a day off. Give yourself and your child a pat on the back.

OTHER WAYS TO EXERCISE

If you go on an outing and walk a lot, this counts as exercise. My wife, Cheryl, and I regularly walk in downtown Chicago and along the lakefront for miles. Our primary intent is to enjoy the scenery and time together, but it's a "fitness" activity nonetheless.

If you have access to aerobic exercise equipment (stationary bicycle, elliptical trainer, treadmill, stair climber, rowing machine, ski machine, aerobic rider, etc.), it can substitute for or be added to the aerobic activities previously mentioned. Be sure that your children are adequately trained and supervised when using this equipment, and participate along with them.

As you progress, increase the intensity of your child's aerobic activity and the difficulty of resistance training about every two weeks. Workouts shouldn't take more than about an hour, included stretching.

Always proceed to the next exercise without resting; fitness trainers call this "circuit training." It helps your child maintain a brisk heart rate and burn more calories.

Chart your progress. Set goals, measure, demonstrate improvement, and set new goals.

I know that one hour—even half an hour—may be tough to find in your family's busy schedule. But isn't it worth your child's long-term health and well-being?

I think I know your answer.

NO GIMMICKS NEEDED

You can do it. You can take charge of your family's health, despite the challenges you face.

You and your kids can get in shape and lose weight. You can feel better and have more energy. You can show your love by staying healthy for each other.

You can reduce your risk of obesity-related problems if you get to work now. But don't think of it as work. Think of it as optimizing your potential, as maximizing your chance of living well. Think of it as being a good example to those around you.

Most importantly, think of it as your response to the God who loves you infinitely. Not that you can pay God back for what He's done for you. But you want to serve Him to the best of your ability, out of gratitude. We're given only one "tabernacle," and we ought to care for it.

There are no quick fixes, no gimmicks, in that effort. It takes long-lasting lifestyle changes. Diet fads come and go, but the common-sense advice in this book has stood the test of time. Even if a "miracle" medicine comes down the pike in the next few years—and don't hold your breath in the hope that it will—you should still follow the guidelines in this book and teach them to your children.

There really is no magic to weight control and fitness; but that's okay, because no gimmicks are necessary. It's all about small changes, patience, and consistency. Your family can return to wholesome eating, daily physical activity, and eliminating junk food and the "couch potato" mentality.

It may not be easy, but you know that anything of value rarely is. Keep a positive attitude. Constantly encourage your child to be the best he or she can be.

Remember that a journey of a thousand miles begins with a single step. For the sake of your kids, and with God's help, it's time to take that step.

IF I CAN DO IT, YOU CAN, TOO

Throughout this book I've included real-life examples of kids and parents who've gained control of weight problems. What about me?

Well, let me give you a few more words of encouragement. At the time of this writing I consider myself to be in pretty good shape for a 46-year-old. My height is 5 feet 11 inches, my weight 165 pounds; my body mass index is a comfortable 23. But it hasn't always been easy. I've had to work hard to stay fit.

Several years ago, after a long history of playing basketball and golf, I was diagnosed with osteoarthritis of my right hip. The pain was debilitating. It came as a bit of a shock to be diagnosed with an "old person's" disease at 39.

My hip arthritis was likely the result of several factors—including a congenital abnormality of my right foot and cartilage breakdown in my right knee. This was all part of a chain reaction of abnormal stress that had moved up my right leg and worn down my hip cartilage. By 2003 I'd reached the end of my "pain rope."

In January 2004 I had a total hip replacement using a minimally invasive approach. I was back at work within three and a half weeks, but complete recovery was slow going. I've now returned to a regular workout routine and am playing golf pain-free.

Despite these difficulties—and mine are minor compared to the burdens some bear—I've been able to stay in shape by working out regularly. Little things—mowing the grass with a non-propelled mower, not using a cart when I play golf, walking constantly at work—help me to stay fit.

The recommendations in this book are ones I follow myself. Do I indulge at times? Of course! But as I see my birthdays fly by, I've had to decrease my intake of food. This is necessary for all of us as we age; if we don't eat less or work out harder, the evidence will soon accumulate.

Lest you think I'm genetically blessed, allow me to fill you in on my family background. My mom has struggled with her weight for years; my dad is in good shape but has a little extra "jiggle" around the middle. Except for my late grandfather, my dad's side of the family has no shortage of weight problems, due mostly to patterns of eating and inactivity.

Let this be an encouragement to you and your children. Heredity and habits don't have to lock you in the obesity trap. I know how hard it can be to overcome both, but I've also seen the rewards in the lives of my patients as well as in my own life. May God bless your efforts, too, as you partner with Him to raise fit kids.

GLYCEMIC INDEX AND GLYCEMIC LOAD

H ere are glycemic index (GI) and glycemic load (GL) values of some common foods, listed in alphabetical order by food type.[1]

The GL isn't available for many foods, but can be calculated by multiplying the total carbohydrate amount in a serving by the GI (example: GI 44 = 44 percent = 0.44 x 20 total carbs = GL of 8.8). GI and GL values vary according to source, probably due to variations in the food tested and methods of preparation; these differences generally are not significant.

TABLE 4

	Glycemic Index	Glycemic Load
Low	Up to 55	Up to 10
Medium	56-70	11-19
High	Over 70	Over 19

FOOD	GI	GL	FOOD	GI	GL
Baked Goods			Healthy Choice Hearty		
Apple muffin	44	10.8	Seven Grain Bread	55	
Blueberry muffin	59	16.3	Kaiser roll	73	
Crumpet	69		Melba toast	70	
Doughnut, cake style	69		Oat bran	50	
Pastry	59		Pita	57	
Scones	92		Ploughman's Whole		
Cakes			Grain Original	47	5.4
Angel Food	67	18.4	Pumpernickel, whole grain	46	6.2
Chocolate with frosting	38	22	Sourdough	54	
Pound	54	13.4	Rye	64	
Sponge	46	16.8	White	70	
Vanilla with frosting	42	26.2	Whole-grain wheat	64	
Cookies			*Breakfast Cereals*		
Butter	47		All-Bran	38	9
Chocolate	44		Bran flakes	74	13
Oatmeal	55		Cheerios	74	15
Peanut Butter	32		Corn Chex	83	21
Shortbread	64		Cornflakes	92	24
Vanilla Wafer	77		Cream of Wheat	74	22
Breads			Crispix	87	22
Bagel, plain	72		Froot Loops	69	18
Bagel, pumpernickel	51		Frosted Flakes	55	15
Bagel, stone-ground			Golden Grahams	71	18
whole wheat	53		Grape Nuts	71	15
Baguette	95		Life	66	16
Croissant	67		Muesli, natural	49	10
Dark rye	76		Oat bran, raw	50	2
English muffin	77	8.4	Oatmeal (non-instant)	48	11
Hamburger bun, white	61		Puffed rice	87	22

FOOD	GI	GL	FOOD	GI	GL
Puffed wheat	67	13	*Drinks*		
Quaker Quick Oats	65	17	Apple juice	40	10.6
Raisin bran	61	12	Cola	65	17.1
Rice Chex	89	23	Gatorade	89	
Shredded wheat	67	13	Grapefruit juice	48	7.5
Special K	69	14	Orange juice	57	12
Total	76	17	Pineapple juice	46	
Wheatabix	75	16	V8 Splash Tropical Blend	47	12.7
Crackers, Pretzels, Popcorn, Chips			Water	0	0
Doritos tortilla chips	42	11	*Fruit*		
Graham crackers	74		Apple	38	
Popcorn, light microwave	55	3.5	Apricot, dried	32	
Popcorn, regular	72		Apricot, fresh	57	
Potato chips	56		Banana	56	
Pretzels	83		Berries (see note below)		
Rice cakes	80		Cherries	22	
Rye crackers	68		Dates	103	
Saltine crackers	74		Fruit cocktail, canned	55	
Water crackers	63		Fruit Roll-Ups	99	
Wheat Thins	67		Grapefruit	25	
Dairy and Soymilk			Grapes	46	
Custard	43		Kiwi	52	
Ice cream	58		Mango	55	
Milk, chocolate	42		Orange	43	
Milk, skim	32		Papaya	58	
Milk, soy	31		Peach	42	
Milk, whole	30		Pear	41	
Yogurt, fruit	36		Pineapple	66	
Yogurt, plain	14		Plum	39	
Yogurt, sweetened	33		Prunes	29	

FOOD	GI	GL	FOOD	GI	GL
Raisins	64		Lentils, green and brown	30	
Strawberries	40		Lentils, red	27	
Watermelon	72		Split peas, yellow	32	
Grains			*Meats and Eggs*		
Barley	25		(see note on next page)	0	0
Buckwheat	54		*Nuts*		
Corn, fresh, on the cob	59		Cashews	22	
Corn, frozen	47		Peanuts	15	
Corn, taco shells	68		Walnuts	15	
Cornmeal	68		*Pasta*		
Couscous	65		Fettuccini	32	
Rice, brown	55		Linguini	50	
Rice, instant	80		Macaroni	46	
Rice, sticky	98		Macaroni and cheese,		
Rice, white, long-grain	57		boxed	64	
Rice, wild, long-grain	54		Ravioli, meat-filled	39	
Rice, vermicelli	58		Spaghetti, boiled		
Rye, whole-kernel	34		5 minutes	33	
Wheat, whole-kernel	45		Spaghetti, boiled		
Legumes			15 minutes	44	
Beans, baked	44		Spaghetti, protein enriched	28	
Beans, black	30		Spaghetti, whole wheat	37	
Beans, butter	33		Tortellini, cheese-filled	50	
Beans, chickpeas	33		Vermicelli	35	
Beans, garbanzo	34		*Soups*		
Beans, kidney	29		Black bean soup	64	8.3
Beans, lima	32		Green pea soup, canned	66	6.3
Beans, navy	38		Lentil soup, canned	44	5.7
Beans, pinto	39		Minestrone soup, Campbell's		
Beans, soy	16		condensed	48	18.2

FOOD	GI	GL	FOOD	GI	GL
Minestrone soup, homemade	39	5.1	Onions	10	
Split pea soup	60	5.8	Parsnips	97	
Tomato soup, Campbell's condensed	52	14.6	Potato, French-fried	75	
			Potato, instant	85	
Tomato soup, homemade	38	2.8	Potato, new, boiled	59	
Vegetables/Root crops			Potato, red, baked	93	
Beets	64		Potato, russet, baked	56	
Broccoli	10		Potato, sweet	52	
Cabbage	10		Potato, white, baked	60	
Carrots, fresh, boiled	51		Potato, white, boiled	56	
Green peas, frozen, boiled	51		Potato, white, mashed	70	
Lettuce	10		Pumpkin	75	
Mushrooms	10		Red peppers	10	
			Yams	54	

Note:

- The way a food is prepared affects its GI and GL. In general, the more "raw" and unprocessed the item, the lower its GI compared to other versions of the same food. The more something is cooked, the more its GI/GL tends to go up, since it's easier to digest it. This is particularly true of legumes and pasta.
- Blueberries, blackberries, raspberries, strawberries—berries of all kinds—are very healthy foods that should be eaten liberally. Values for most berries, however, were not available.
- Meats and eggs contain few or no carbohydrates—thus a GI/GL of 0.

FIBER VALUES OF COMMON FOODS[2]

Fiber figures differ according to the source, but this will give you a good base of knowledge. Assume we're dealing with average-sized pieces of fruit.

FOOD	FIBER (grams)	FOOD	FIBER (grams)
Cereal/Grains		Cereal, Cracklin'	
Bran, miller's	11 per 1/2 cup	Oat Bran	12 per cup
Bread, white	1 per 2 slices	Cereal, Fruit 'n Fiber	8.5 per cup
Bread, pumpernickel	2.6 per 2 slices	Cereal, Multigrain	
Bread, seven-grain	6.5 per 2 slices	Cheerios	3 per cup
Bread, whole-grain	3-6 per 2 slices	Cereal, Post Fruit and	
Buckwheat	4.8 per 1/2 cup	Bran, Peaches, Raisins,	
Cereal, All-Bran	10 per 1/2 cup	and Almonds	6 per cup
Cereal, Atkins Brand		Cereal, Post Raisin Bran	8 per cup
Blueberry Bounty		Cereal, Post Spoon-	
with Almonds	9 per cup	Sized Shredded	
Cereal, Cheerios	3 per cup	Wheat 'n Bran	6.4 per cup

FOOD	FIBER (grams)	FOOD	FIBER (grams)
Cereal, Wheaties	3 per cup	Grapefruit	1 per 1/2 grapefruit
Oatmeal	14.4 per cup		
Popcorn	1 per cup	Grapes	1 per cup
Rice, brown	2 per 1/2 cup	Green beans	2 per 1/2 cup
Rice, white	0 per 1/2 cup	Honeydew melon	1 per cup
Rye, 100 percent	14.9 per cup	Lettuce	0.4 per 1/2 cup
Whole wheat, 100 percent	15.2 per cup	Mushrooms	2 per 4 large mushrooms
Dairy Products	0	Orange	2
Fruits/Vegetables		Peach, fresh	2
Apple	2.8	Peaches, canned	2 per cup
Apricot	1	Pear	6
Artichoke	4.5	Peas	4 per 1/2 cup
Asparagus	1.7 per 1/2 cup	Pineapple	0.8 per 1/2 cup
Avocado	3 per serving, 1/5 avocado	Plum	1
Banana	2	Prunes	2 per 3 prunes
Beets	2.5 per 1/2 cup	Raisins	1 per tablespoon
Blackberries	3 per 1/2 cup	Raspberries	4.6 per 1/2 cup
Blueberries	2 per 1/2 cup	Sauerkraut	1.5 per 1/2 cup
Broccoli	3 per 1/2 cup	Spinach	7 per 1/2 cup
Brussels sprouts	2 per 1/2 cup	Strawberries	3 per cup
Cabbage	2 per 1/2 cup	Tangerine	2
Cantaloupe, 1/4	1	Tomato	4
Carrots, cooked	2 per 1/2 cup	Turnip greens	2.6 per 1/2 cup
Cherries	1 per 10	Watermelon	2.8 per 1 thick slice
Corn, sweet, on the cob	1 per 4-inch piece	*Legumes*	
Cucumber	0.7 per 10 thin slices	Beans, baked	9 per 1/2 cup
		Beans, kidney	7 per 1/2 cup
		Beans, lima	4.4 per 1/2 cup

FOOD	FIBER (grams)	FOOD	FIBER (grams)
Beans, navy	6 per 1/2 cup	*Pasta*	
Beans, pinto	5 per 1/2 cup	Bella Vita, low-carb	
Chickpeas	6 per 1/2 cup	Penne Rigate	8 per 3/4 cup
Lentils	3.2 per 1/2 cup	Hodgson Mill Brand	
Nuts		whole wheat spinach	
Almonds	3 per ounce	egg noodles	5 per 2 ounces
Cashews	1 per ounce	Macaroni	1 per cup
Chestnuts	7.3 per 1/2 cup	Spaghetti	1 per cup
Peanut butter	1.1 per tablespoon	Whole wheat spaghetti	4 per cup
Peanuts	2 per ounce	*Potatoes*	
Pecans	3 per ounce	Baked, with skin	3
Pine nuts	3 per ounce	French-fried	1 per 10
Sunflower seeds	2 per ounce	Sweet potato	4 per 5-inch potato
		Yams	6.8

CALORIES BURNED BY COMMON ACTIVITIES

Here are calories burned in a 125-pound person per 1/2 hour of the activities listed.[3]

ACTIVITY	CALORIES BURNED PER ½ HOUR	ACTIVITY	CALORIES BURNED PER ½ HOUR
Aerobics	165	Rollerblading	210
Basketball	240	Running, medium pace, 12-minute mile	240
Bicycling, 12-14 miles per hour	240		
Cross-country skiing	240	Stairstep machine	180
Golf; walking, carrying clubs	165	Swimming	210
Jumping rope	300	Tennis	210
Lawn mowing	135	Walking, brisk, 17-minute mile	120

Note:

- A 1-ounce bag of potato chips and a 12-ounce can of pop each contain about 150 calories. You'd need to jump rope continuously for half an hour just to burn those calories!

- These values vary depending on the person's size and gender, and the intensity of the activity. These are averages for an adolescent boy or girl at about 125 pounds.

CALORIC REQUIREMENTS FOR CHILDREN

Here are daily caloric requirements for children of various ages, based on the National Academy of Sciences Food and Nutrition Board.[4]

	0-6 month old	7-12 month old	12-24 month old	3-8 year old	9-13 year old	14-18 year old
Male	570	743	1046	1742	2279	3152
Female	520	676	992	1642	2071	2368

Note:

These are average caloric needs for an average child with average activity levels. Depending on your child's size, muscle mass, and activity levels, the above may vary considerably.

NOTES

Introduction

1. Finkelstein, Eric, et al, "State-Level Estimates of Annual Medical Expenditures Attributable to Obesity," *Obesity Research,* 2004, 12:18-24.

2. "Childhood Obesity," *Postnote,* Parliamentary Office of Science and Technology (UK), September 2003, Number 205.

Chapter 1

1. Farooqi, I. Sadaf, et al, "Clinical Spectrum of Obesity and Mutations in the Melanocortin 4 Receptor Gene," *New England Journal of Medicine,* 2003, 348(12): 1085-95.

Chapter 2

1. Sbarbati, Andrea, et al, "Obesity and Inflammation: Evidence for an Elementary Lesion," *Pediatrics,* 2006, 117 (1): 220-223.

2. Lyon, C.J., et al, "Minireview: Adiposity, Inflammation, and Atherogenesis," *Endocrinology,* 2003, 144(6): 2195-2200.

3. Sinha, R., et al, "Prevalence of Impaired Glucose Intolerance Among Children and Adolescents with Marked Obesity," *New England Journal of Medicine,* 2002, 346(11): 802-810.

4. Erickson, Sarah J., et al, "Are Overweight Children Unhappy?" *Archives of Pediatrics & Adolescent Medicine,* 2000, 154:931-935.

5. Strauss, Richard S., and Pollack, Harold A., "Social Marginalization of Overweight Children," *Archives of Pediatrics & Adolescent Medicine,* 2003, 157:746-752.

6. Latner, J.D., and Stunkard, A.J., "Getting Worse: The Stigmatization of Obese Children," *Obesity Research,* 2003, 11(3): 452-456.

7. Eisenberg, Marla, et al, "Associations of Weight-based Teasing and Emotional Well-being Among Adolescents," *Archives of Pediatrics & Adolescent Medicine,* 2003, 157:733-738.

Chapter 5

1. Ball, S.D., et al, "Prolongation of Satiety After Low Versus Moderately High Glycemic Index Meals in Obese Adolescents," *Pediatrics,* 2003, 111:488-494.

Chapter 6

1. Rask-Nissilä, Leena, et al, "Prospective, Randomized, Infancy-Onset Trial of the Effects of a Low-Saturated-Fat, Low-Cholesterol Diet on Serum Lipids and Lipoproteins Before School Age: The Special Turku Coronary Risk Factor Intervention Project (STRIP)," *Circulation,* 2000; 102(13): 1477-1483.

2. Sondike, S., Copperman, N., and Jacobson, M., "Effects of a Low Carbohydrate Diet on Weight Loss and Cardiovascular Risk Factors in Overweight Adolescents," *The Journal of Pediatrics,* 2003, 142: 253-8.

Chapter 7

1. For more information on dietary fiber, see the wonderful little book by Betty Kamen, Ph.D., *New Facts About Fiber* (Novato, Calif.: Nutrition Encounter, Inc., 1997).

Chapter 8

1. From the Centers for Disease Control, National Center for Health Statistics, at www.cdc.gov/growthcharts.

2. Adapted from the National Institutes of Health Obesity Education Initiative Classification, available at www.nhlbi.nih.gov/guidelines/obesity/prctgd_c.pdf.

3. Cook, S., et al, "Prevalence of a Metabolic Syndrome Phenotype in Adolescents: Findings from the Third National Health and Nutrition Examination Survey, 1988-1994," *Archives of Pediatrics & Adolescent Medicine*, 2003, 157(8): 821-7.

Chapter 9

1. Castro, L.C. and Avina, R.L., "Maternal Obesity and Pregnancy Outcomes," *Current Opinion in Obstetrics and Gynecology*, December 2002, 14(6): 601-606.
2. I list just two here, but an Internet search will keep you busy for hours:
    a. Armstrong, J., and Reilly, J.J., Child Health Information Team, "Breastfeeding and Lowering the Risk of Childhood Obesity," *The Lancet*, 2002-6-8, 359:2003-2004.
    b. Hediger, M.L., Overpeck, M.D., and Kuczmarski, R.J., et al, "Association between Infant Breast Feeding and Overweight in Young Children," *Journal of the American Medical Association*, 2001, 285:2453-2460.
3. Lucas, A., Boyes, S., Bloom, R., et al, "Metabolic and Endocrine Responses to a Milk Feed in Six Day Old Term Infants: Differences between Breast and Cow's Milk Formula Feeding," *Acta Paediatr Scand*, 1981, 70:195-200.

Chapter 10

1. Mrdjenovic, G., and Levitsky, D., "Nutritional and Energetic Consequences of Sweetened Drink Consumption In 6 To 13 Year Old Children," *The Journal of Pediatrics*, 2003, 142:604-10.

Chapter 11

1. Greer, Frank R., and Krebs, Nancy F., "Optimizing Bone Health and Calcium Intakes of Infants, Children, and Adolescents," *Pediatrics*, 2006, 117:578-585.

2. Ibid.

3. American Academy of Pediatrics, Committee on Nutrition, "Calcium requirements of infants, children, and adolescents," *Pediatrics,* 1999, 104:1152-1157.

4. Lloyd, T., et al, "Lifestyle Factors and the Development of Bone Mass and Bone Strength in Young Women," *The Journal of Pediatrics,* 2004, 144:776-782.

5. van der Mei, I.A.F., et al, "Past exposure to sun, skin phenotype, and risk of multiple sclerosis: case-control study," *British Medical Journal,* 2003, 327:316-20.

Chapter 12

1. From www.WorldofQuotes.com, Historic Quotes and Proverbs Archive.

Chapter 13

1. Strong, William B., et al, "Evidence Based Physical Activity for School-Age Youth," *The Journal of Pediatrics,* 2005, 146:732-737.

2. Thomas Jefferson, edited by Eric S. Petersen, *Light and Liberty: Reflections on the Pursuit of Happiness* (New York: The Modern Library, 2004), 13.

3. "Policy Statement on Strength Training by Children and Adolescents," *Pediatrics,* 2001, 107:1470-1472.

Chapter 14

1. Field, Alison, et al, "Relation Between Dieting and Weight Change Among Preadolescents and Adolescents," *Pediatrics,* 2003, 112:900-906.

2. Kleinman, Ronald E., editor, et al, *Pediatric Nutrition Handbook* (Elk Grove Village, Ill.: American Academy of Pediatrics, 2003), Table C-1, 921.

3. Saarilehto, S., et al, "Growth, Energy Intake, and Meal Pattern in Five-year-old Children Considered as Poor Eaters," *The Journal of Pediatrics* 2004, 144:363-367.

Appendices

A. Compiled from several sources, including www.glycemicindex.com and the article by Kaye Foster-Powell, et al, "International Table of Glycemic Index and Glycemic Load Values: 2002," *American Journal of Clinical Nutrition*, 2002, 76: 5-56.

B. Compiled from several sources including the following:

    a. Betty Kamen, Ph.D., *New Facts about Fiber* (Novato, Calif.: Nutrition Encounter, Inc., 1997).

    b. Pennington, Jean A.T., and Douglass, Judith Spungen, *Bowes & Church's Food Values of Portions Commonly Used* (Baltimore: Lippincott Williams & Wilkins Publishers, 2005).

    c. Netzer, Corinne T., *The Complete Book of Food Counts* (New York: Dell Publishing, 2003).

C. Compiled from the following sources:

    a. www.fitresource.com

    b. www.calorie-counter.net.

    c. Harris, Dan R., editor, *Fitness and Exercise Sourcebook* (Detroit: Omnigraphics, 1997).

    d. Sharkey, Brian J., Ph.D., *Fitness & Health* (Champaign, Ill.: Human Kinetics Books, 2002).

D. Kleinman, Ronald E., et al, *Pediatric Nutrition Handbook* (Elk Grove Village, Ill.: American Academy of Pediatrics, 2003), Table C-1, 921.

Note: Listing of Web sites does not constitute blanket endorsement or complete agreement by Focus on the Family with information or resources offered at or through those sites.

FOCUS ON THE FAMILY®

Welcome to the family!

Whether you purchased this book, borrowed it, or received it as a gift, we're glad you're reading it. It's just one of the many helpful, encouraging, and biblically based resources produced by Focus on the Family for people in all stages of life.

Focus began in 1977 with the vision of one man, Dr. James Dobson, a licensed psychologist and author of numerous best-selling books on marriage, parenting, and family. Alarmed by the societal, political, and economic pressures that were threatening the existence of the American family, Dr. Dobson founded Focus on the Family with one employee and a once-a-week radio broadcast aired on 36 stations.

Now an international organization reaching millions of people daily, Focus on the Family is dedicated to preserving values and strengthening and encouraging families through the life-changing message of Jesus Christ.

Focus on the Family Magazines

These faith-building, character-developing publications address the interests, issues, concerns, and challenges faced by every member of your family from preschool through the senior years.

| Focus on the Family **Citizen®** U.S. news issues | Focus on the Family **Clubhouse Jr.™** Ages 4 to 8 | Focus on the Family **Clubhouse™** Ages 8 to 12 | **Breakaway®** Teen guys | **Brio®** Teen girls 12 to 16 | **Brio & Beyond®** Teen girls 16 to 19 | **Plugged In®** Reviews movies, music, TV |

FOR MORE INFORMATION

 Online:
Log on to www.family.org
In Canada, log on to www.focusonthefamily.ca

 Phone:
Call toll free: (800) A-FAMILY (232-6459)
In Canada, call toll free: (800) 661-9800

BP06XFM

More Great Resources
from Focus on the Family®

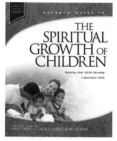

Parents' Guide to the Spiritual Growth of Children
General Editors: John Trent, Ph.D., Rick Osborne, Kurt Bruner
Passing on a heritage of faith to children is an incredible privilege God gives to parents. And now there's a tool to help make it easy! Inside the *Parents' Guide to the Spiritual Growth of Children,* you'll find dozens of simple, practical ways to develop Christian values and make faith in God part of everyday life.

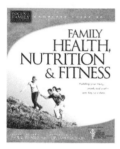

The Complete Guide to Family Health, Fitness and Nutrition
by Dr. Paul Reisser
Who knows your children's sniffles and sneezes better than you? Now take family care-giving to a whole new level with this comprehensive, easy-to-use reference book. In-depth appendices and reference sections provide the most current and reliable medical information available to help you know when to call the doctor.

Why ADHD Doesn't Mean Disaster
by Dennis Swanberg, Dr. Walt Larimore & Diane Passno
Why ADHD Doesn't Mean Disaster provides a realistic, encouraging perspective from parents who have raised children with ADHD, as well as some who have ADHD themselves. Filled with insights, personal stories and sound medical expertise, this book gives parents facing the challenges of handling ADHD hope that breaks through the hype.

FOR MORE INFORMATION

 Online:
Log on to www.family.org
In Canada, log on to www.focusonthefamily.ca.

 Phone:
Call toll free: (800) A-FAMILY
In Canada, call toll free: (800) 661-9800.

BP06XP1